MW01717256

Praise for *Fourteen Hills*

"Beautifully designed, impeccably edited, *Fourteen Hills* is one of those handful of literary journals doing the important work of keeping American writing alive and new."
George Saunders, author of *In Persuasion Nation*

"The journal is something of a collage itself, boasting a variety of talented writers from San Francisco and around the world."
Jennifer Gomoll, *NewPages.com*

"[*Fourteen Hills*] blends the traditional litmag with experimental writing in a slick, well-produced journal."
Todd Dayton, *MetroACTIVE*

"Smart, quirky, literate—every piece in this journal gives the reader a juicy nugget to sink their teeth into, and something meaty that sticks to the mind's ribs."
David Henry Sterry, author of *Chicken*

Fourteen Hills

THE SAN FRANCISCO STATE UNIVERSITY REVIEW

Vol.20 No.1

2014

Acknowledgements.

Fourteen Hills would like to thank the following for help and support in putting this issue together:

Maxine Chernoff
Jennifer Daly
Barbara Eaton
Karl Frauhammer
Glass Door Gallery
The Booksmith
Genevieve Lowe
Michelle Matson
Gregory Miller of Gregory R. Miller & Co. Publishing

Fourteen Hills would like to thank the following businesses and individuals for their generous donations to our fundraising events:

Cafe Royale, Maxine Chernoff, Mark Danielewski, Dandelion Chocolate, Diesel, Funky Door Yoga, Good Vibrations, Hey Cookie, Humangear, Kelli Eng, Lucero Salon, Pierced by Tony, The Rumpus, Subpar Miniature Golf, Susan Calvillo, and Trader Joe's.

Credits.

Book Layout and Design: Monique Mero-Williams
Cover and Art Design: Melton Cartes, Jennifer Lewis and Monique Mero-Williams
Copy Editors: Matthew Heitland, Patrick Johnson, Ari Moskowitz, Ryan Nash, Shadia Savo, and Kendra Schynert
Cover Artwork: Marilyn Minter
"It's Mine"
2007, Enamel on Metal

Distribution.

Small Press Distribution, Berkeley, California / www.spdbooks.org
Ubiquity Distributors, Inc., Brooklyn, New York / www.ubiquitymags.com

ISBN: 978-188929261-8

Fourteen Hills is published by the Creative Writing Department at San Francisco State University, with the support of the Instructionally Related Activities Fund.

Fourteen Hills

THE SAN FRANCISCO STATE UNIVERSITY REVIEW

Vol. 20 No. 1

2014

Fourteen Hills is published twice yearly in San Francisco, California.

Subscriptions:
Individual – One year for $15. Two years for $28.
Institutional – One year for $17. Two years for $32.
Single issues $9.

Writers may submit once per submission period. All submissions are electronic. Submission periods are: September 1 to December 1 for inclusion in the spring issue (released in May) and February 1 to June 1 for inclusion in the winter issue (released in December). All other correspondence may be addressed to the appropriate editor at *Fourteen Hills*, c/o the Creative Writing Department, San Francisco State University, 1600 Holloway Ave., San Francisco, CA 94132. Details at www.14hills.net.

Contents.

Fourteen Hills

THE SAN FRANCISCO STATE UNIVERSITY REVIEW

Brief Abandon

Lucy Burns

In the after bloom
of our love
I find canaries
small wild birds
rushing from my
throat, informants,
they sing my thoughts
in blurred images
finches who left
the coastal,
mountainous
regions of my body
peck your face
until it bleeds
yellow. Desperate
they flit from sheet
to crumpled pillow
dodging your waving
hand. I can't stop
you from opening
the window, can't
stop them from
flying away. I
hold the last bird
in my mouth
breathe its feathers
suffocate its song.

The Women of America's Secret City in 1945[1]

Jeannine Hall Gailey

Seated politely in plaid skirts and hot-rollered hair
at the controls of calutrons, having been warned

by a billboard on the way to work: "What you see here...stays here"
are told they have helped America win the war.

They are not yet concerned about uranium, the cemestos
(concrete and asbestos) walls of their assigned rental homes,

the effects on their skinny children selling comic books of "Atomic Men"
for five cents on the side of the road. A generation later

my father would walk these same buildings with dosimeter,
talk to dying janitors, build robots who might spare

their lives. Design concrete caps to protect us from decay.
The women he worked with every day were friendly, contained

like the particles under the K-25 and Y-12. My childhood of barbed wire and warning
signs at the fishing holes, the simmer of seventies protest versus patriotism,

had none of that obedient beauty: the horned-rimmed chemists and physicists
unquestioning in sensible heels the yearly x-rays, the uranium taped to their wrists.

---

[1]Thanks to photographer Ed Westcott, whose photos inspired this poem. The pictorial is available online from The Atlantic: http://www.theatlantic.com/infocus/2012/06/the-secret-city/100326/

Labor Day

Ivan Hobson

In the hotel pool at sunset
I saw that dragonfly
still on the water's edge.

I offered a finger as a raft,
waded the two of us towards the sagebrush
near the shallow end.

When I was young my fingers knew
they were meant for threading needles,
untying small knots, touching my mother's face.

They understand metal now, machine dials,
nicks from lathe chips and grinding wheels.
They have grown used to force and friction.

They are no longer scared to save the drowning,
to hold and set the spiders free outside the door.
There is nothing they want to harm.

They are just not as nimble.
Offering the safety of a branch,
accidently tearing a wing.

Migration

Ivan Hobson

Near the Pacific Ocean
hundreds of Monarch butterflies flutter
in and out of sunshine, the canopy
of the eucalyptus grove around me.

Such a long way from home,
the machine shop being auctioned next month,
the workers that were once so sure
of the iron they milled

finishing their final shift tonight,
pulling up the collars on their wool jackets
and puffing out into the cold.

The full moon will be soft against the wings,
the boot prints left in the snow by the rank and file
before the gates are locked for the last time.

How long have there been migrations?
Families like ours leaving collapsing towns,
fluttering hundreds, sometimes thousands of miles.

So many beings finding, or trying to find their way.

Workmen's Compensation

Dustin M. Hoffman

Indications: For the temporary relief of ten-hour days, including: demoing triple-layer shingles, spreading rosin and nailing shingles, or spreading tar or rolling rubber. Will ease shame of your denied raise, neglect of your grid's perfect symmetry. Paychecks will miraculously appear without scabbed kneecaps and a kinked spine, sunburned scalp and aching ankles. You can wear sweatpants or underwear or nothing at all during daylight instead of jeans hardened in tar. You will decrease proximity to the sun, and daylight will become full of opportunity. More time, time, time.

Directions: A hammer will do. A hammer balanced on top of your ladder ready to fall when you hoist it against your chest. Or stand past the safety step, or allow the feet to slide, or use that hammer to bash the safety stop: these are just a few ladder options. Here's another: prolong stares at your coworker, Camille, straddling the peak, stretching to nail cap, revealing the olive skin on her lower back. Daydream about fucking against hot shingles, bending her over the fresh porcelain in the half bath, lifting her body against the cinder-blocks of the basement. Relax, remember to breathe, and let the ladder do the rest.

Active Ingredients: Gravity, cudgel, fear of OSHA, disorientation, daydreams and fantasies, aluminum, mineral spirits, nailer, worn sneaker tread, desire.

Side Effects: Days may appear longer at home. Too long. Vitamin D intake drops when your blinds are always closed. Paranoia induced by the man wearing the hard hat who drives slowly past your window, who snaps pictures when you peep through the slats. You cannot understand why he wears a hard hat while driving. Try blinking to make sure your vision is clear. He may be out to catch you, he may be out to kill you, he may become something like a coworker if you bring him coffee, but remember to suck air through your teeth, clutch your side. Or, just stay inside and think of Camille. Think of her knocking on your apartment door, begging you to come back, because no one else asks about her big plans for the weekend, about her six-year-old son's Tee-ball game. No one else can make her happy. But only consider; don't envision. Avoid hallucination. Avoid hallucinating hard hats.

Directions: Stepping on a nail is not enough. Prolonged disablement is your goal. But not permanence. The balance between lasting and forever is delicate but essential. The eave borders are easy to forget when working backwards, a quick slip over fascia and soffit. Your fall must appear accidental, but remember to plan. Combine falls with pine trees or shrubs, compost piles or full dumpsters. Land on legs, and not your neck. Practice on your mother's gabled ranch that your father built but didn't have time to re-shingle before dying. When the time comes, a one-story roof will not be enough, and three stories are too much. Remember to cry for Camille when you land. Remember to groan. Use your diaphragm. Choke and gurgle through your punctured lung.

Consult Doctor: If erections last longer than four hours. If Camille never appears at your threshold but never leaves your mind. Seek holistic treatment: lubricant, callused grip, Camille's kerchief, magazines, movies. You have time now. Go to the bar and drink and drink. Go to the bar and buy drink after drink for the woman who will lean on your shoulder, squeeze your bicep, sneak you into the women's bathroom. If ejaculation does not erase desire, do not return to work. Several days and shifts and weeks and months may pass before you lose feeling. You have plenty of time for Camille to fade. Consider compounding your claim into emotional distress.

Side Effects: The man in the hard hat will drive by and snap pictures at dawn, your old punch-in time. He creeps up to your front door. You watch him through the peephole, and all you see is hard hat. It is white, a sticker of the American flag pasted on the stubby bill, part of it scratched away to fuzzy gum. When you open the door carrying Pop-Tarts, he has disappeared. Only the white hard hat sits on your front step, and you have no use for that. He will not be your friend. You realize you're not as close to your coworkers as you thought. They do not call, do not visit. You will long for their voices bounding over the ridge, will long for the swoon of a fresh bucket of tar, for the flesh of plywood turned black and sparkling, for the simple clarity of chalk-line grids. Resist. Resist these small satisfactions from the time when you worked for the hour. Enjoy your clean fingernails, your peeling skin, the paleness underneath. Seek distraction. Get a hobby. Boats in a bottle, astrophysics, sea monkeys, pottery, but no roofing.

Storage: Keep in a cool, dry place. Avoid direct sunlight, or even the indirect sunlight squeezing through the cracks of your blinds; you've earned shadows. Stay away from windows and hard hats. Remain indoors. Sign up for direct deposit, an option before impossible when you cashed the wrinkled checks your boss scratched out in his third-grade cursive, numbers the bank teller squinted at, asked her manager to confirm, too much cash to place in your grease-stained palms. Avoid interaction, questions, chitchat and philosophy. You and Camille talked about starting your own roofing outfit and supernovas and circumcisions and underwater caves and skipping out of work like you used to skip out of high school. You and her, crawling across the rosin, swinging your legs over the rake and onto the ladder, then off to the beach to fry. Forget the conversations that made you sweat. Replace with the rattle of your air-conditioner.

Indications: Your pottery is lopsided but don't call it failure. You'll learn to enjoy the higher arts. Reassess the caving lid on the vase you name *Mother,* the lopsided plate you title *Father* before kneading it back into a ball, the sunbaked ashtray shaped like a diamond you consider leaving at Camille's front door. You know she smokes but not where she lives. Now you have time to gain real knowledge. Improve your mind. Read the encyclopedias your father bought when you were five that still consider Pluto valid, that end the presidents at Ford. You've lugged them to every new home and now there is time. Don't visit your mother or succumb to the guilt of her leaking roof. Guard your precious hours and blame your spine, your fractured shin, your sprained wrist, your emotional distress. She may be the root. Just look at that caving vase. Crush that ashtray. Don't think about Camille. Stop trying to face the man in the hard hat.

Directions: A hand slipped in hot tar is a start, but the whole cooking bucket dumped across your legs is more effective. Avoid your lap, which may lead to erectile dysfunction. Pass, for once, on drinking the cans of Coors Camille doles out after lunch. Your claim could be threatened by inebriation. Listen to the empties plink over the eave and fight your dry tongue. Drink water. Chug your gallon warm as piss from sitting in the sun. Your gallon that once held milk, then water, the jug that looks identical to the one where your boss stores mineral spirits. Drink mineral spirits. Your nights at the pub, shots of Jameson lined up across the oak bar, they were all practice for this. Open your throat, swallow, and then hack. Blame improper storage. Unlabeled spirits that burned the tar off your hands and now burns your esophagus. You won't need your voice when you have time.

Side Effects: Rectal bleeding, uncontrollable vomiting, a liquid diet. What goes in must come out. Difficulty swallowing, like shingles in your throat. Swollen tongue, oral blisters, inarticulation or complete inability to speak. But silence is not all bad.

Excuse: It's not that you won't answer your mother's calls about the mold, the puddles in her carpet, you can't.

Excuse: If you found Camille's home, showed up at her door, it's not that you wouldn't know what to say; your tongue can't form the words.

Exclusion: When the man in the hard hat whispers through your vents at night, quizzes you with his questionnaires, you don't have to lie. You shake your head, shiver and blink, curl your fingers and toes, but he can't read what you mime. He can't see through the blinds and the garbage bags you duct-taped over the windows. He relies on his ears sprouting from under his hard hat, and you can't explain.

Consult…dead father, sodden mother, pretend lover. They will not hear you. There is only you and the man in the hard hat who has taken to sleeping in his van in your parking lot. His hard hat has changed to blue, bobs over his brow as he breathes deep. You strain a whisper through your gravelly throat, through the slice of his cracked window; coax him, the power of somnambulistic suggestion. You are ready to return to work, to Camille, to ladder rungs and rooftops. You plead. But have you had enough time? He checks boxes in his sleep, his pen waving over his clipboard to the rhythm of his gentle snoring. Three more months of compensation. You beg for a stack of shingles balanced over your shoulder, but you will remain weightless. Why can't you just enjoy extra time?

Side Effects: You were advised to ignore your mother's mossy shingles, but here you are, lugging your cast over the peak. The trouble is the ladder, how long it takes you to carry up shingles, to carry your broken body. The trouble is the silence of working alone, no distraction; time flattening out and spreading like rolls of black rubber. The trouble is no Camille. You take three times as long to secure the drip edge, to sculpt the valley, to bend the flashing. And you can't discover the leak, the weakness left by your father. You slog on, cooking your new pale skin. Your mother pushes sunscreen; you've never needed it before. How many red blisters must sprout before the man in the hard hat drives by and sees you are able? He abandoned his stakeout at your apartment complex, and he doesn't show up here, at the home your father built, the shed with the single forty-five degree slope where he aimed the BB gun at your thigh to show you how the neighbor's dog felt. Shot in the leg, and you still had to mow the lawn. No escape from work. Now, no man in the hard hat to see your work, to send you back.

Directions: The nail gun provides accuracy. Stigmatic left hand or foot looks bad but heals quickly, and there's always the right. Disengage safety catch so nails can fire without surface pressure. Camille will do one of her pretend hold-ups: "Gimme all your flashing, or else." You raise your hands to the sun and smile. She squints, shakes away strands of loose bangs, quick draws the nailer and aims for your chest. Without the catch, the nail releases. You watch its painfully slow trajectory. Enough time for Camille's eyes to pop, lips to spread. Three inches of galvanized steel buries into your chest. Three inches are plenty to pinprick an organ. Ignore the Spanish that spills from Camille like a sparrow shrieking in a cat's jaw. Ignore the creases in her forehead, her quivering hands, the dropped nailer that somersaults over the eave, the sound of plastic shattering on concrete. Camille has freed you. Camille's fingers feel you, squeeze your breast, press a blue kerchief into your wound.

Inactive Ingredients: Safety catch, calluses, trust in the tools you know, guilt, prayer, emergency room, the doctor's pliers so much shinier than any tool you've ever held, your sun-burned body.

Storage: Rest in soft places. Seek comfort. Couch to recliner to bed replaces truck bed to five-gallon bucket to roof cap. At the end of your last fourteen-hour shift, you and Camille collapsed on the freshly shingled roof, watched, on your backs, dusk paint the clouds pink. No pitch could tip you. After so many hours on tilted ground—thirty degrees, forty-five, sixty—gravity changes, bodies acclimate to angle. Impossible to fall. Now you require zero degrees. Flat and soft and alone and yet you worry this flat world will swallow you.

Symptoms: Have you forgotten all that time can do for you? You drag the utility blade across your cast, sprinkling the carpet with white flakes all evening. At twelve dollars per hour, you would have made forty-eight dollars, but why are you calculating? You no longer work for hours, time cards, crinkled personal checks, don't need to. Your leg underneath the cast is pale, shrunken, streaked in blood where you pushed the knife too deep. You tear the bandages from your chest, scrape the blackened scab, long for the shiny nailhead Camille planted there. You drink a beer because you are thirsty and you're sick of water and milk. Your throat burns. You call your own answering machine and practice listening—to your own voice, to any voice, saying, *I feel better. I'm ready. I'm sorry.* You play the message over and over and wonder if those tin-can words are really yours.

Interactions: The man in the hard hat no longer stalks you, but you've tracked him down. Your gift of time was spent this way, circling, hunting Camille. And when you couldn't find her, you found him, the man in the hard hat's van parked on a hill. He is not inside, but two hard hats lie stacked on the passenger's seat—a white one, his blue sleeping hat. You lean on his bumper and stretch your arms, pink and raw from re-shingling your mother's roof. Your skin betrays you, leaks heat, and fall is here, then winter and snow and no more roofs. The hill overlooks a new subdivision on one side. On the other side, the flat black rubber roof of apartment complexes. Homes and houses. Leases and mortgages. All the roofs you can see are fresh, perfect. But a roof must be rotting somewhere.

The man in the hard hat appears through the pine trees. Binoculars and a camera tangle on straps around his neck. His hard hat is bright red. He doesn't see you until he is yards away. He raises his binoculars, gazes off at a framing crew in the subdivision over your shoulder, ants to you, busy and industrious and swinging hammers, climbing ladders, shooting nailers. You pick up a pebble from the road, throw it at the man's red hard hat. It plinks, and he keeps peering through the binoculars. You throw more pebbles. Nothing will stop his search, his work. You try to yell at him and choke. You try to charge him and stumble. Your chest stings with each palpitation.

The man in the hard hat aims his binoculars directly at you, and now is the time to show him your hammer, how you can still swing it, lift shingle stacks, climb any ladder. But you are too close. You are a blur crouching on the ground, coughing up blood.

Overdose: Watch for the symptoms. Listless shifting from couch to bed. You carry your hatchet hammer, pound nails into the apartment walls, yank them out. Experience agnosia. More and more black holes pierce the white walls, but there is always more white. Snow outside, snow mounded on your mother's roof, probably mounded on Camille's roof, wherever she lives. You touch yourself but can't remember her skin over the shingles—anorgasmia. All the white and soft drowns the sound of hammer throws, of your mumbling, of your wanting to clink up the ladder and return to a work that is hibernating. The pleasure of time may lead to avolition, anhedonia, Antarctica, and another hour, and another. Turn on the TV, relax your fingers, and let your hammer go. Ignore the mute thump of steel hitting carpet.

Busbound Hulk

Matthew Fogarty

My ticket lists a seat number but the seat's already taken—three men on a bench meant for two—and all the other seats are taken too and there's a crowd of men and women and children standing in the aisle of the bus. The long mass of riders behind me continues the push even once I'm as close as a twin with the families amassed behind me. There's no room in the overheads for my pack—they're all full up with bundles and bags and packs and cases—and so I loop the strap around my leg and set it on the floor. There's a rising heat of arms and sweat-soaked hair and cotton, a mutual grasp for stable air. I'd thought this would be a good way to see the countryside but all I can see is the visible stench of the breath of the man next to me, his lips at my ear, whispering rot. Were this trip any longer, I would fear we'd all become fused together, fused into one busbound mass, fused even to the bus, the bus a megahuman then, superhuman, with brains and limbs and lungs, heartfull. This is how monsters are formed, I think, in tragic sci-fi tales about human-and-sheet-metal hulks that, despite their excess of ventricular flesh and muscle, know nothing of love.

Carpet Shop

Farzana Marie

For Khorshid, *whose name means "sun"*

It's always the sandals that are left on the scene,
thrown from a suddenly-airborne body,
spit like a watermelon seed.
Hers were fuchsia, with flowers,
and landed near her chalk drawings:
purple Cupid-pierced hearts
smeared now.

It was Saturday, sunny,
when she was blown up
in front of the carpet shop
on Great Massoud Road.
She and three kids who spent afternoons
working new moves at Skateistan,
or hawking trinkets and practicing English
with soldiers walking between camps.
She and her eight-year-old sister.
She and the carpet shop owner,
blown into shards of flesh
by a fourteen-year-old in a vest.

I didn't hear the blast.
I was 7,846 miles away,
brushing my teeth before bed
maybe, or blowing out a candle.
Someone later sent me pictures
of the scene of the attack,
knowing I'd lived in that camp
by the carpet shop,
not knowing I'd lost her in those pictures.

And yet she was never mine except
for the way she would run to me, except
for our snapshot, her pink jacket tucked in close,
smiling from my Facebook page.

Warnography

Farzana Marie

War's like love.
It finds a way.
Why should it ever end?
— Bertolt Brecht, *"Mother Courage"*

I was too young once not to dream of you,
you in the magazine under my pillow,
the alluring cover a smooth
M249 SAW propped on ammo-can,
camo'd face squinting, slightly blurred
beyond the bold, slick barrel.
That was before I knew you.

The sirens you dispatched to lure me
changed their tone once we got closer,
Kandahar Airfield's robotic yet sultry
screech through sleep after a "thud, thud"—
Rocket. Attack. Rocket. Attack.
Move to nearest shelter and take cover.
Rocket. Attack. Rocket. Attack.
Our acquaintance was still casual in those days.

But Sangin was where I finally saw you naked.
You promised action, yeah,
that was the one promise you kept,
in your twisted way—
and not just to me, to all of us.
Murder holes. Check.
IED traps. Check.
Slug-fest firefights. Check.

You took and took.
What did you give?
You didn't tell me how it was
with your other lovers.
I didn't know,
I didn't used to know
how it looked
when it ended.

The Lucky

Patricia Canright Smith

> *...Ah, whom can we ever turn to*
> *in our need? Not angels, not humans*
> *And already the knowing animals are aware*
> *That we are not really at home in*
> *our interpreted world.*
>
> —Rainer Maria Rilke

On November 5, 2003, Arthur Simpson slipped off the granite dome at Remarkable Rocks, Kangaroo Island, Australia, and plunged 150 feet into the Southern Ocean. No one saw it. Finally his wife, Sandy, picked her way around the crocodile jaws, which were orange, coated with a vibrant moss/mold found only here. On the cliff side, she spotted a head in the sea below and she screamed. Two men from a tour bus grabbed a rope; they slid and bumped down the rock to perch on a promontory, where they repeatedly hurled a flotation device. But the rope was short, the device flimsy, their footing uncertain: a monstrous wave pulled them in as well. Forty minutes later another tremendous wave washed Arthur, still breathing, still conscious, onto a different rock ledge. A helicopter winched him up.

Here's what to do with a large, healthy, 54-year-old man who has been thrashing about in frigid waters for almost an hour: get his clothes off quickly, but very gently, as though he could shatter, because when the heart is that cold any jolt can make it stop. Place hot packs under the arms, on the chest, neck and groin; wrap him in blankets and pump warm, saturated air into the nose.

Arthur says he's sleepy not cold. Then he asks, how long? Not too long, they say, and he asks again. Not too long.

Arthur kept asking until he dozed off. Sandy knew he wanted the precise number of minutes he was in the ocean; the Advanced Care paras thought he was asking how long to the hospital.

In the emergency room they rewrapped him in warm flannel blankets, fed him warm sweet tea and delivered warm saline through an I.V. That evening, when Arthur was finally out of danger—even hours later, the heart can stop—they told him how lucky he was. More than lucky. It was a miracle. They did not mention the two men who drowned.

~

He's *glaring*—really, the day after he almost died and we're back to this? Of course we are. Because Arthur hates to wait, so I should have been here at the crack, never mind I didn't get back to the hotel until after midnight and I've had to call ten million people.

How are you feeling, sweetie?

How do I *think* he feels? Vertigo, a vicious headache, a broken nose, crinked neck, aching knees, weeping abrasions on his temple, thighs, arms, elbows, and hands, and the ocean screaming in both ears.

So much for commiseration. No one feels sorry for Arthur.

He tells me a Dr. Foxall, who actually looks like a fox, finally showed up at 8:18. Heart, lungs, nose, abrasions, it all looks okay, he just has to take it easy. No way to do a brain scan so I'll have to keep watch: excessive sleep, or, you know, if I can't wake him.

Arthur didn't like it either. He proposed Adelaide, but oh no; no flying for seven days, he has saltwater in the middle ear, from the force of the waves and the gasping. Which explains the dizziness. And that sound that's driving him bat-shit.

No, Dr. Foxall said if we took our scheduled flight later today—he said *shed-dooled*—both Arthur's eardrums would burst. Arthur had to question that. The little 340 turboprop did not go much above eight thousand feet on the flight in. So then the doctor said, all friendly-like—you know, just two guys having a pint?—*like two ice picks stabbed into your brain, yeh?*

So we're stuck. For a week. I try to put a happy face on it: Look, you're up, you're dressed, you're being discharged! You're *alive*. Which elicits the look. Oh, I see; we're not going there. But seriously, he could have—by all rights he *should* have died. He is just astonishingly lucky.

Finally, Arthur says sorry. I wait. He says sorry again. He says he is disappointed about the itinerary, is all. He has a hard time thinking of himself as lucky.

That's my husband. I have never been able to picture him as an artist. Was that it? Maybe architect, I forget. Back in the 70's, his first life. His second life he was an adventurer, filmmaker and photographer. Now he's running Power Solutions, the family business, third life, which is when I came on board. I wonder, after this is he going to start on a fourth?

This is my first life, and what a mess. Well, not totally. The girls are good, I have my shop. But I have to figure out what I'm doing with my marriage. I am not getting any younger.

As I pack up toiletries and the bag of damp clothes I tell Arthur about this morning's *Islander*, "a tragic twist of fate," they called it, that the rescuers—apparently a Scottish tourist and a local tour-operator—were "*swept* into the turbulent waters and *drowned* by the *very waves* that proved to be the American visitor's *salvation* as he was washed onto a *ledge beyond the clutches of the sea*." Can you imagine that in the New York Times? I say. Then I look at him. Oh, God, didn't he know?

Oh, I'm sorry, I say. It's not your fault, Arthur. I lean over and try to hug him around the bandages.

I've never ached for Arthur, not after his divorce—well, of course not then, we were in love—not after his motorcycle accident, not after his mother got cancer. Not even during the Power Solutions scandal. But right now, I do. Poor guy.

Finally, I straighten up and say, Hey, you're not the only disappointed one, bucko, I was planning on procuring some serious Barrossa Valley wine this week. Now what am I supposed to shop for?

He doesn't even look at me. I feel completely inadequate. Silence makes me tense and I say stupid things.

The speed limit here is fifty, not thirty-two, Arthur informs me in his FYI voice. He is painstakingly peeling tape from the metal thing on his nose.

I am driving on the wrong side of the road, I say. I am being careful. What are you doing?

I don't need this thing.

Right, he's the doctor. Though he's probably right. It's not like he's going to crash into something with his face. Arthur actually isn't accident prone, though he definitely is not cautious. Balls-out, he calls it. I hate that expression. It gives me a gross visual image; makes me want to shout; Do you mean *big hairy balls*?

I say, Budget did make driving sound perilous.

They were jerks.

Tourists, they informed us, and we took that to mean *Americans*, are not accustomed to sandy surfaces sporting the odd large marsupial, so they inevitably *slam on the brakes* and the vehicle invariably *hydroplanes into a ditch*. Those Aussies have a way with words. *Going bush*. You would think every customer they'd ever had has "gone bush." Arthur suggested the problem wasn't tourists, it was the *Rodeo Sport*, the only car they had *on hire*. But they were right about the marsupials. We saw a bunch yesterday, all dead.

Arthur, I say, but he interrupts.

Sandy, did you see me fall?

Ah. The "mistake." Arthur hates mistakes. Never mind the nightmare we went through, never mind my having to watch him flail for an *hour, every second* thinking he would not come back up. I take a deep breath.

I didn't, I say. I didn't even realize you had gone around to the other side.

If I had realized he was headed that way would I have said something? It's unbelievable: a smooth-as-glass granite dome with a 150-foot drop and they have no fences, no barriers, nothing. Well, a polite little "Danger" sign. But what would I have said, Careful, dear? Arthur never listens to me. And I was distracted by that lady in the tangerine hat trying to get herself off the bus.

Reminds me of Baja, he says. Same sky.

Mmmm. So does Kangaroo Island also have whales?

He went to Baja to kayak with gray whales. I skipped that trip. I usually don't go anymore. I only came on this one to be the Wife for the

ConSol dinner in Sydney. Good thing.

He looks wretched. The gauze turban doesn't help. God, when he was in the water—it was *insane*. All I could think about were all the times I had fantasized about him not coming home. Like this was some kind of karma. Like it was my fault. It makes me want to throw up.

Where's Birds of *Australia*?

Packed, I think. In the back. You want me to stop and get it?

No thanks. Then he says, Where's my Moleskine notebook? That notebook is like his best friend.

I don't—when did you have it last?

He is staring out the window.

Did you have it at the Rocks?

I'm trying to think, he says. Damn. It's got everything in it, twenty years. No, more like thirty. Twenty-eight. Seven.

I'll stop.

No, don't. I don't want to know. Then he says, Funny how something beautiful can become tainted. Now this place seems almost ugly. Like everything's been washed with gray.

That's interesting, I say, and I smile. Then it occurs to me—does he mean me? Have I become washed with gray?

This fucking drive is taking forever. Was this Hansen Bay Cabins the only place you could find?

I glance at him. I can't help sighing. Can't he ever just go *along*?

Well, shit, I want to know.

One of the nurses recommended this place and boom, she had the owner on the phone. What was I supposed to do? It's near Flinders Chase. (Flinders Chase is the reserve we were headed for yesterday when we stopped for a quick look at Remarkable Rocks.) And she said they have nesting fairy penguins. I thought you would like that.

Arthur is a collector. He has "life lists," not only for birds but for mammals, fish, insects, mollusks, I don't even know what all. He was happy about getting marsupials. I don't think fairy penguins are a marsupial, though. They must be a bird, but I am not going to ask.

You look like you're walking a tightrope, he says.

I am driving on the wrong side of the road, I say. There are dead kangaroos everywhere. It's creepy.

The fairy penguins are at Hansen Bay, or Flinders Chase?

Oh. I thought she said Hansen Bay.

Did you cancel the place near Adelaide?

Tanonga Luxury Suites. I left a message.

The swim with the dolphins outside Cairns?

Done.

He lays his head back against his folded-up fleece and looks out the window.

So what do they have at Flinders Chase? I ask.

Without lifting his head he says, Tamar wallabies, heath monitors, bush-tail possums, echidnas, koalas, platypus, and one emu, the only one on the island.

He sounds watered-down.

One emu, I say. Must be lonely. I would love to see an emu.

He says it bums around the parking lot. People feed it.

You doing okay? I say.

He doesn't answer.

Over the next hour, Arthur reports two big soaring raptors and some type of eagle. At Murray's Lagoon—he remembers the name; I doubt he's brain-damaged—he says, Five white ibis, two stilts, and a shitload, too many to count even at your speed, Sandy, of little grebe-like ducks.

I guess since he has no way to write them down, I get them.

He says, This reminds me of driving with Mom in her Caddy.

It's the *wrong side of the road*, I say. Shut up, I think.

At the Eleanor River, seventeen Cape Barren geese in the sedge. When I ask if he'd like to go down to see the seals at Seal Bay Tourist Centre, he says, Are you kidding? Jesus.

Going over Kelly Hill we finally have to stop so he can puke. It must be shock, or the vertigo. Arthur doesn't get carsick, but of course he's always the one driving.

At the turnoff to Hansen Bay, he says, I haven't spotted a single cockatoo. And no marsupials, either, except dead ones. They just leave them there along the roads. Terrible.

He sounds so wistful. We've got time, I say. As if I can cheer him up.

~

On November 6, Arthur and Sandy checked into the Hansen Bay Cabins. There was no receptionist, no manager; they found the key under the mat, as per instructions, and let themselves in through the back door of #1. It was off-season, and they were the only visitors.

"Hansen Bay Cabins" are four joined, white-painted units, a one-star motel crossed with a Boy Scout bunkhouse set on a bare concrete slab on a bare red-dirt knoll in a vast landscape of knobby bushland. White molded-plastic chairs, two per unit, sit in front of each aluminum screen door. They overlook a deserted, pristine bay and the Southern Ocean, which extends uninterrupted to Antarctica. A dirt path and some crumbling concrete steps lead down to a horseshoe beach strewn with rocks and bleached driftwood. The sea brings to mind postcards of the Mediterranean, but Hansen Bay is cold.

There were no shops. No market, no restaurant. Except for the wooden shed behind the cabins, there were no other buildings at all, just the miles of low-growing, gray-green scrub threaded with red-dirt veins. Most visitors come to savor the serenity of the place. Some find it healing.

~

Pretty, isn't it?

Is that a joke?

Oh, he means the beach. He's right, that could be the prettiest little bay I've ever seen. I would love to find a textile with those colors— cerulean, aqua, almost celadon at the edges.

So this place is not tainted? Oppressive?

Arthur considers. He raises his shoulders—ouch!—and says, It's okay.

Well, good, I say. Because the last civilization was thirty kilometers ago at Vivonne Bay, thirty *dirt-road* kilometers ago. I look at my cell phone. Though we may need to go there if we want contact with the world.

Arthur nods. He looks woozy.

I say, Let's get you back inside, Buster, and he immediately clutches my arm and leans on me as though he's been waiting for an offer. I have to swallow hard. I have never thought about what it might be like when Arthur gets old.

The "cabin" is fine, Aboriginal prints, slate floor, wooden tables and chairs. It smells stiff and lemony. Two bedrooms, twin beds with heavy plaid bedspreads, and Arthur goes for one while I unpack. I hate being out of touch, not only for the girls, but for my shop. And okay, for Jeff, though I promised myself I would not talk to him on this trip. I seriously have to figure out what I'm doing. Which is what I've been saying for, what, two years? Limboland.

I tiptoe into the bedroom. Arthur seems to be asleep. I'm supposed to wake him every hour. I look at my watch. I gather *The Horse Whisperer*, my water bottle, and a plaid wool throw—hoo-ha, somebody here really likes plaid—and head out to the white plastic chairs. The concrete is warm on my feet, and the sun and breeze—like marzipan, so sweet it almost hurts my cheeks. I lean my head back and close my eyes. I forgot that it would be spring here.

Arthur appears and says he can drive.

I must have fallen asleep. It takes me a minute.

But it will get dark before you can get back, I say. Thirty kilometers on these dirt roads takes, like, an hour-and-a-half, right? And Budget said not to drive after dark.

Oh for Christ's sake, Sandy. I'll take it easy.

You saw all those dead kangaroos.

Sixteen.

Really? That many?

Sixteen.

No.

No what?

No, you're not driving to Vivonne Bay. All seriousness aside.

Not even a chuckle. Well what are we going to eat, then?

I have no idea, Arthur.

Did you *know* there were no restaurants out here, Sandy?

I really didn't think about restaurants, Arthur. Forgive me if I was more concerned with finding a comfortable place for you. Let us never forget that it's all about *you*.

Our eyes are locked. But I am being mean to a man who almost died, a man whose bruised, piercing blue eyes are strangely opaque, whose handsome face is oddly slack. Oh god, I am tired. A long night, a long drive, a horrible two days and I am so tired.

Arthur glances down at his hands and pokes at the gauze. He looks up and gazes at the sea. After a few moments, as though nothing has happened, he says, The foam on the waves looks like cake frosting. It's the angle of the light. Then he says, Ten second intervals. No gulls. Huh. I'll have to look that up.

After a moment I say, You know, they said "self-contained." Think that might mean food?

Arthur looks in my direction, but like he doesn't see me. He flips open his cell phone. You're right, he says. No service. But, again, his tone is not annoyed, it's mild-mannered. Like Clark Kent.

Shock. Of course that's it. I do not want to even consider brain damage.

I pull stuff from the cupboards while Arthur recites: Cadbury biscuits, one; "XXXX Bitter," whatever that is, *six*; Heinz baked beans, *four*; Heinz stewed tomatoes, *four*. Carnation condensed milk, *one*.

Check, I say: Arm & Hammer baking soda, *check*, Medura Tea, *check*. Salt and pepper, cinnamon, curry powder, oregano, parsley, thyme. Tabasco. *Check*.

We are laughing. We stand in the kitchen and look at each other. It's been a long time.

I'm so sorry, Arthur.

He shrugs, says Christ, I *must* stop doing that, and chuckles again. He picks up one of the beers and reads: "Fourex refers to the tradition of using x's to denote the strength of the brew. Castlemaine, Victoria, since 19-and-24." I could use maybe eight x's, he says. So what do you want to do, girl?

I look in the little fridge. How about a cold XXXX? I hold out a beer. And we can make eggs and beans and eat it out on the lanai, or whatever they call it in Australia.

He looks at the bottle and then at me. Will you join me? he says.

I drink wine.

Sure, I say, Sure I will, babe.

In the morning, I make eggs and beans again, throwing in the stewed tomatoes. Arthur looks so much better, less pale, less shell-shocked, and without the gauze turban he has his beautiful curly hair back. He's moving better, too.

I ask, Does a flat square of frozen white bread sound good to you? Because I can't find anything that looks like a toaster.

He laughs.

Interesting names, he says when I join him outside. He's found a wildlife book. They call albatross "mollymauk." Then he says, I really wanted to see the fairy penguins last night, but somehow my vision wasn't right. And I couldn't get going, like my body was not under my control. Don't know what that's about. I probably should have insisted on a scan.

We could still go to Adelaide.

Two ice-picks stabbed into my brain? I think not.

Okay, now I am officially worried. It is not normal that Arthur doesn't want to go to Vivonne Bay. He doesn't care about messages? I can get whatever looks good to me? He even said no to Flinders Chase, his one objective here. He claims he's just tired—but I have never heard Arthur say he's tired, not once in ten years. Something is wrong.

I go out to the porch and sit down.

He says, They spend all day out there. It takes them fourteen hours to amass the calories they need for their own nutrition plus the babies, the majority of which they burn just keeping warm. Not the most efficient system.

He is rotating his head very slowly, left to right, his eyes still on the sea.

I watch the waves. I push up my sleeves and sunbathe my arms. I tell him again I *am* glad he didn't die. He says he doesn't want to talk about it. I am glad he didn't die. Maybe he thinks…oh, who knows what Arthur thinks. Who ever knows?

I wonder how many calories I burned, he says. Then, Maybe at dusk. The babies smell the parents coming in and start calling. I'm sure that's what I heard last night. The burrows must be down in those rocks, or up in the mallee.

He sounds like Mr. Rogers talking about the neighborhood. I am trying to stay upbeat but this mild-mannered thing is freaking me out. Disappeared, like Forrest Gump. I need to call that doctor. Arthur is not himself.

Can you think of anything else we need? I say. I should probably get going. I need to check in with my sister and the girls.

He doesn't answer.

Finally I say, Come on, Arthur. What's up?

Did you hear the penguins last night?

What time last night? After we went to bed?

He fiddles with the bandage over his elbow. A *huhn-huhn* sound, he says. You wouldn't call it a quack or a honk, more like a humming expiration. The long moan you do when you're sleeping.

I moan in my sleep?

No, I do. Wakes me up sometimes. You didn't hear anything? It was hard for me with these ears.

Oh, I forgot about—do they bother—is there something I should get?

He shrugs and winces. Just have to wait, he says.

Is that what you're doing? I say. Waiting?

Maybe I should sit and wait with him. We can talk about penguins.

Soak in the sun. Eat beans one more day. I could just hold his hand and keep him company while he stares at the sea. Ten years has to count for something.

I don't know. Sandy, I just wonder what happened. I have this blank space.

So you're trying to remember?

Well. I wasn't, but when you ask…I was thinking about the penguins, actually.

Right. But there's something else. Maybe you're not thinking about it but it's there.

Something I'm not thinking about, he says. He stares at me for a minute, then back at the ocean. He scratches the back of his hand around the gauze.

Want me to stay here with you? I could go to Vivonne Bay tomorrow.

That's right, there is something else. That I'm not thinking about. Thank you, he says.

I say, Well, you did—

Do not say I *almost died.* I did *not* almost die. I knew I would not die, every minute I was in that water, I knew. And it was terrible, Sandy, it was the worst thing I have ever been through, just *appallingly* cold and I was choking and puking and being pounded by waves that felt like slabs of wood, and still I knew I just had to get through it. And I knew I would. I am not that guy who drowns while vacationing in Australia.

For some reason this makes me want to cry. I say, But maybe while you were *falling* you thought you would die. Maybe that's what's bothering you.

Arthur shakes his head, ow. He says, Actually, I would say that I am not myself, but I would not say that something is bothering me. I wouldn't put it like that.

How would you put it?

I would say I am not myself.

Well doesn't it bother you, to not be yourself?

He's thinking it over.

No. In fact it doesn't. I find it…interesting. I am not *myself.* Think about that, Sandy. It's a kind of freedom.

Arthur is scaring me. Something is scaring me.

What can I do? Arthur, I don't know what to do. *I* thought you were going to die.

Arthur sighs. I'm sorry, Sandy. I really am.

And that's all I'm going to get. Maybe that's all there is. I stand up. I take a step, and then I hover behind him. The sea is mesmerizing, surging over ivory sand and hissing out. Abruptly, Arthur points at a rocky ledge above the cove.

Look. See that?

What? Where?

Look, just watch, he says. He is gingerly turning his head. He says, wow, they're everywhere, and he points. Look, look, he says. Out there, behind the car.

He always wants me to see whatever-it-is.

And then I do see one. A little brown lump not much bigger than a cat slow-hops from one shrub to another and hunkers down, and even though I know it's there, I can't see it. Then I see another one, blump blump. They are everywhere.

Penguins? I say.

Tamar wallabies, he says. They don't have them on the mainland. How about that. He looks pleased.

I look at him; I mean, really look. Maybe he *is* happy. Maybe Arthur loves all this, maybe it is making him feel better, maybe it's more than just adding to his list. Maybe it always has been. Sandra Lee, just how well do you know this man—and why don't you know him, why haven't you taken the effort to know your own husband? Or gotten out, one or the other. You loved him and then it got tough and you just let it go, just moved into a bigger house and decorated the hell out of it. A grown woman settling for a free ride, it is simply ridiculous, a ridiculous way to live. You were a *designer*, you had a *plan*. Is it somehow easier to waste your life? And his, too, for that matter. It's more than ridiculous, it's reprehensible.

I lay my hands on Arthur's shoulders, very gently. They feel strong and warm. My stomach tightens: remember Arthur's wonderful shoulders?

They're adorable, I say. Slow little humps, like little claymation creatures. I love how they appear out of one shrub, hop to the next, and then just dissolve. Crawling all over the—what do you call it, Arthur?

Topographically, this is a coastal plain, he says, so you could call it a plain. Or scrubland, or bushland.

I feel happy. Because we are on a coastal plain, but you could call it scrubland or bushland. Because of these darling little wallabies. Because Arthur seems cheered by the wallabies. Because I am cheered by the wallabies and I am cheered by Arthur. Because it is spring here, which seems to be making me sad.

What are they doing? I say.

I would guess they're eating, honey. Living off the land, it's what animals do. Find food, make babies, take a rest. These guys can even drink salt water if they have to.

I rub his neck very gently. You sort of make your living off the land, too, I say.

Right. By fucking it up.

Don't be like that. Isn't ConSol clean energy?

Arthur doesn't answer. I sit down again and put my hand on his.

Arthur says, Did you get a look at the other two guys?

What two guys? I say. I am confused. Because we are watching wallabies. We are talking about wallabies, I am thinking about wallabies.

What two guys? I say again.

The guys that tried to rescue me.

My stomach plummets. *How could I have forgotten those two men?*

No, I say. I mean, yes, I did watch them go down the cliff and then I didn't see what happened, I just—those horrible waves, I was watching *you*, Bunny, I had to keep my eyes on *you*, I had to hold on to your little head—

Arthur says mildly, My head is not little.

—and every time you went under I had to make sure you came back up. Why was the sea so stormy? It was a beautiful day, why were the waves so big? And there was nothing I could do. Tears sting my eyes and I take off my sunglasses to wipe.

Finally I say, So that's what's bothering you? Those guys?

He says, I saw one of them. At first they were just, you know, figures throwing a buoy. It wasn't even close and I was fighting the water. But then I saw a head, not more than twenty feet away. Between the waves, I saw his head. I saw his eyes—we saw each other.

We sit for another hour. We watch the sea. It is too sad, those men.

Arthur counts twenty-eight wallabies. He finally he convinces me to head out to Vivonne Bay. He pats my hand and says You're a good girl, Sandy.

It always used to make me so mad when he called me a good girl, though for the life of me, I can't remember why.

~

On November 7, Arthur Simpson stood on the concrete porch of his rented cabin at Hansen Bay watching the sun approach the Southern Ocean's hazy horizon. He stripped off his clothes. Supporting himself on the rusted metal handrail, he crept barefoot down the crumbling cement stairs to the beach.

At dusk, his wife, Sandy, returned from her excursion to Vivonne Bay and carried in the groceries. She looked around the cabin and then went out front, where she found the clothes. She strode through the cabin a second time, searched the two bedrooms and the bathroom again, and then strode back to the porch, where she shielded her eyes and searched the beach. She jogged down to the beach. She stood on the sand, scanning.

Behind her, she heard a *huhn-huhn* and she whirled around. A yellow beak jutted from a hole in the rocks. *Huhn-huhn. Huhn-huhn.* More beaks appeared, like two-inch chopsticks with bent ends. A tiny torpedo washed up with the surf, popped to its feet and began waddling toward the rocks as if Sandy were not there. *Huhn-huhn-huhn.* Two babies rushed out, *huhn-huhn-huhn-huhn-huhn-huhn,* and the mama crammed her beak into their open mouths and coughed up dinner.

Sandy scanned the sea again. The penguins must have drawn him to the beach, but into the water? Her legs felt shaky. Was there a rogue wave?

Then, in the deepening dusk, Sandy thinks she sees something bobbing just beyond the breakers, maybe a deadhead, or a dolphin, or a sea lion. Or a swimmer.

Arthur, she calls. *Arthur*. Please come in now. Honey, it's time. The little penguins are here.

Seed With Rice

A. Anupama

When lovers lie on a bed, and embrace each other so closely that the arms and thighs of the one are encircled by the arms and thighs of the other, and are, as it were, rubbing up against them, this is called an embrace like "the mixture of sesamum seed with rice."
— from *The Kama Sutra of Vatsyayana*, tr. by Sir Richard Burton

This beaded curtain
is made of grains of rice strung
like jasmine flowers, tied gently with
loops of impossibly fine thread
and seeds of sesame, each one pierced through
its center with a very thin needle
and the same fine thread.
Impossible to see through,
and when you touch it
you must touch gently, it is so delicate,
parting as you move fingertips first,
then your face and shoulders,
brushing your skin
gently, gently,
rice and sesame seeds on threads
hanging from the doorframe
of the other room
with perfume of jasmine.

Lise H----Leaves A. Renoir
To Marry Henri T---, June 18, 1879

Mimi Plevin-Foust

Ask me why.

Can I pack you a lunch? He puts down the brush.

Just ask me.

He kisses her cheeks.
Morning light rinses
her shoulder, her skirt.

Auguste— She shakes her head.

Light showers her, color from the garden
spattering her hat and bag—
almost like Claude's portrait of Camille
on her deathbed—
the skin worked in strokes
crumpled as the sheet's.

She lifts her valise, Well, then—good-bye.

He wipes a sleeve across his eyes.
The canvas shimmers.

The soft period begins.

103°

Mimi Plevin-Foust

When we met you gave me a cactus—
baby saguaro with a red flower
I left home.
In three weeks you said we'd kill this crop
and have plenty cash to kiss Los Altos
good-bye—seven weeks now
we're still picking.

Reach-snap-drop my shoulders burn
the basket drags my waist my back
aches to snap.
You lose at blackjack half the night
and sweat me up till dawn.

Sal says one pair of big arms
is as warm as the next
but she never rubbed my feet
after work; she never sang me "Silent Night"
in August—

Now you nudge me as I stare through the vines
at more vines   *Look alive girl*

I dream what it must be like
to feel cold—what a frozen river
must look like
glass
as I skate between its banks like a bird.
That speck I skate toward
and away from   is you.

The Monkeys in the Fable

Rodney Wilhite

Seems like we were sent to the creek to fetch water
because her stepfather didn't pay the bill. The bucket
is too heavy so we carry it between us.
Without her glasses she can't even see the stars
that so enchant me. Unlike me, she is not bewitched
by the beauty of the night. I trip over every root,

slip in the mud. We're like the monkeys
in the Chinese fable, I say, sent by the Emperor
to catch the moon's reflection in a pail of water.

    What the fuck are you talking about?
It's dark enough
I can't see her, but know we're walking in step
to avoid sloshing the water. The Emperor in the fable
dispatched his monkeys to cheat death, but I'm no good
    at this, not in the dark.

Bottomland

~

Michael Jones

The men dove off the porch
when shots splintered the door
behind them. Jimson tall
as cotton hid them well.

Jellies of a girl's heart
spittled the door's stripped wood.
Hornets stirred, smelling blood.
The men held on to dirt.

The Trenches

Terita Heath-Wlaz

It’s spinal tap day.
The sun floats into the sky, a giant blood cell.

Birds awaken from dreams of a beetle jackpot.
Gravely, your spoon pierces a soy Junket.

I tell you my assignment from Dad
is getting your pants on. *To you*, I add. Dumb.

You practiced befuddlement at the pew,
told us death was wafer-plain.

Now my ear traps your frantic bleat for God
like a hit of pond water.

Painstakingly, we accomplish the pants.
Your frailty deserves another whole poem.

This poem is about a spoon
carving scallop shapes into a cup of Junket,

and bearing the wet slabs of custard
to your tongue.

Luminous

~

Trina Gaynon

I paint with my back to the world.
— Agnes Martin

mandala of geometry grid shimmering

light turned inward burns itself out
a short loop reveals danger beyond

ego the empty mind easier to make
eye contact with the dead crowding

gallery with noise beyond nature
stretched into grids graphite lines

speaking of her art discomfort blurs
face out of focus still as her hands

pale bands of color uninterrupted

The best things in the world happen to you when you're alone.

I use to meditate before I learned tostop thinking.

Inspiration calls and you have
to take the blame for that.

You get shaken between inspiration
and the final product.

With Such Sudden Heat

Mary Julia Klimenko

he took my breath. I knew that
stranger walking out
the door those restless eyes the smell of corn fields
where everything is flat and forever I imagined I was the first
keeping one eye on that distant water shimmering at the end
of the never ending
road blackbirds, wheeling and turning back on myself
I don't want revenge I want to fly
heat lightening a thousand birds tatter my sleep I know
the silence of rooms as quiet as my grandmother lying in her coffin
hands folded as if she had wings covering her breasts
motionless forever an electric reminder
that heaven is indifferent I want to wake up to stop
falling red silk is me leaning in the doorway
if he doesn't come out of the rain by midnight I'll leave
the door unlocked it's too late to ask his name
nothing matters but my mouth his hands
stroking my thigh skin against rain a woman alone at midnight
standing in the doorway open to all possibilities.

Carnal Knowledge

Kevin McLellan

CARNAL	KNOWLEDGE
between thumb and	index finger on
my palm	the water glass
the mouth	broke
the penetrating	a reminder
a crescent wound	exposed
—	my writing
hand	can't wait
must stay	on the page

Interview: Michael Alenyikov

Ari Moskowitz

Michael Alenyikov's first book, "Ivan and Misha," won the 2011 Northern California Book Award for Fiction and was nominated for the Edmund White Award for Debut Fiction. He is the very proud recipient of the 2013 Gina Berriault Award and has been a MacDowell Fellow. His writing has appeared in The Georgia Review, Descant, The James White Review, New York Stories, Modern Words, and the Gay & Lesbian Review; and has been anthologized in "Best Gay Stories, 2008," and "Best Gay Stories, 2011." He grew up in the outer reaches of New York City's three outer boroughs (and yes, there is an Avenue Z in Brooklyn on the shores of Gravesend Bay). Between the Bronx and Brooklyn, he lived in Phoenix, AZ and Los Angeles, CA. He has worked as a bookstore clerk, clinical psychologist, cab driver, and writer on interactive media projects. In 1989-91 he was on the Board of Directors of the Gay & Lesbian Alliance Against Defamation. After living chunks of years in Syracuse, NY, Boston and Cambridge, MA, and Manhattan, he has made San Francisco his home for the past twenty years. He is one of the one million Americans who suffer from the neuro-immune disease, Myalgic Encephalomyelitis (often called Chronic Fatigue Syndrome), which has crushed the lives of so many people, including countless writers and artists.

Michael Alenyikov is not as well known as he should be. I admit that I had not heard of him before Peter Orner recommended that I read Alenykov's short story collection, Ivan and Misha. Though the collection won the 2011 Northern California Book Award, and deservedly so, Michael Alenyikov is not a household name. As this year's Gina Berriault Award winner, Michael read from his collection to a full room at SFSU's poetry center. I hope that with some recognition in *Fourteen Hills* and with a new novel in the wings, more people will have the pleasure of reading Alenyikov's work.

Michael Alenyikov's command of character in Ivan and Misha is nothing short of brilliant. The stories peel back the layers of each character, and the deeper Michael goes with them, the more he explores their flaws and anxieties. His characters are people; they transform and change as Michael's stories hum along. They are flesh and blood, prone to mistakes, misfortune, and inner-turmoil, as all of us are. But they are more than the sum of their pain. They share moments of great tenderness and joy as well. I asked Michael how he pulled this off. Did he take real people in his life and fictionalize them or alter them in some way so as to make them fit for the page?

His simple answer: "No, with the exception of one of the characters."

I had the pleasure of sitting and talking with Michael in his 1st floor apartment in the Castro. When I came over, his space was exactly as I imagined: a computer on a desk near the center of the room, some bookshelves, and scattered paper. Alenyikov's space is not particularly tidy. He's been there for years and it looks very lived in. But somehow it is just right. His apartment is the space of a man who spends all his time putting the specific details of life onto the page. It's little wonder that he has time for little else.

*

Fourteen Hills (14H): How old were you when you decided to dedicate yourself to your writing?

Michael Alenyikov (MA): Mid-40s.

14H: And you hadn't written in a significant amount of time?

MA: I hadn't written any fiction other than a detective story in the 6th grade. I'd been working as a writer in NY, developing a specialty in interactive media projects. People had always told me I was a great writer, but the kind of writing I was doing wasn't that creative. It was veering in the direction I wanted to go but I still lacked the nerve. I'd given up my career early as a clinical psychologist. I'd driven a cab in Boston and then took a seven week film-making intensive at NYU, which led me to the interactive media work. The event that gave me the chance to write fiction finally was falling ill with Myalgic Encephalomyelitis (unfortunately better known as Chronic Fatigue Syndrome.) Being that sick, I had already decided that film was out of the question. I saw a flyer for a writing class and figured for the first time in my life I wasn't working, so I had free time.

14H: How much research went into the stories in your collection, Ivan and Misha?

MA: Almost none. I'd had to get translations for the Russian phrases I wanted to use; I'd looked up names of Kiev subway stations; I'd gone online to find just the right painting from the Hermitage for a poster to hang in Ivan's apartment. One of the things I love about fiction writing is how you can get something wrong and find a way to still work with it. For example, in my novella, "Sorrow's Drive," there's a scene in Iowa where I describe summer cornfields as yellow and I riff on that color. A friend noted that cornfields are green. I had a moment of panic, then called a cousin in Indiana and managed to still use what I'd written about yellow but make the scene more accurate. In "Barrel of Laughs," near the end when Louie is on a date with Estelle, there's a smell in the air, some flower. I was vague about it, then on revising decided I had to be more specific. I have a friend I met in a writing class back in the '90s. She's a landscape gardener. It's the very end of spring, you're in Brighton beach, what would you smell? I asked her. She's from the northeast: She said lilacs.

M.E./CFS causes a kind of brain damage that waxes and wanes and I learned early on that it's easier on my brain to write fiction where I'm making stuff up than it is to research an article or essay. I can do that extra research and logical organizing, but it quite literally "hurts" more. With fiction, I can just work with my imagination and do a little bit of due diligence when needed.

14H: Did you come from a story-telling background?

MA: The only person who told stories in my family was me. I did not come from a storytelling background. I come from a very unhappy, rather traumatized family. I used to tell stories to friends about my family, building them up into myths with heavy dollops of black humor. It kind of saved my sanity. I used to be jealous hearing of southern writers who picked up storytelling from an uncle or grandmother on the front porch. I'd be really jealous. My family mostly just complained about things. It was kind of grim. My mom died when I was twelve. I think she might have told me family stories and been an all around more interesting person if I'd gotten to know her better. It's one of the tragedies of my life that I didn't get to know her better. And she really encouraged my reading; she even signed me up for a playwriting class. I don't know why she enrolled me in that class, but she did. The last day, we were supposed to bring a draft of a one-act play. I didn't do it, I didn't go. I clutched. And she died a month or two later. We'd migrated to L.A., where she died, and then returned to Brooklyn. I had a sense of retracing that early move when I moved from Manhattan to San Francisco for my health, during a year the M.E. was in remission. But moving back to California, I relapsed after a few months. It took a year before I accepted that I wasn't going to be able to go back to work anytime soon. One day I saw a flyer for a writing class; it was one of those shit or get off the pot moments: if you don't do it now, that nagging sense of dissatisfaction that's eaten away at you all these years, you'll carry for the rest of your life. I don't think I'm at all unique in that grabbing at the chance finally in mid-life and taking the plunge.

14H: I had a conversation with a friend, that the best way to get writing was to get really sick. Was the illness almost a blessing?

MA: Ha! I don't want to get too Northern CA, but it was. Something I've been thinking about too: when I was in college, the first two years I was a math major, and we had to take German and I think it was my fifth semester of German and my teacher knew how to actually teach American students to read German. I have a memory of reading a Thomas Mann short story that was a sketch for what became The Magic

Mountain. I had this recurring fantasy that I'll be able to be an artist when I'm in a wheelchair and disabled, that's what it's going to take. I was envisioning a room in the Swiss Alps with my meals being served and great views, a blanket covering my legs . . . I mean you never know what's going to happen but I assume that if I hadn't gotten sick, I would have stayed in New York and worked hard at a job and never written fiction. With the economy what it has been, I'd likely be unemployed now trying to figure out how to pay the rent on my fifth floor walkup apt. on W. 89th St.

14H: What's your advice to aspiring writers who don't get sick?

MA: You have to find the time to do it, somehow. I read about and hear about and know writers who get up at five in the morning, two hours before work, and that's where they do it, but I'd never be able to do that. And there are writers who write in between changing babies' diapers, writing on the bus or subway to work. MFA programs are a chance to spend two or so years when all you do or think about is writing. But the key is to spend just enough time on a project to keep it alive in your unconscious. That may be you write every day, once a week, a few scattered hours a month, but it has to be active on some level for your creative unconscious to surprise you with an image, a direction, a word that unlocks the story when you're in the shower, just falling asleep, etc.

14H: You don't have a regimented schedule?

MA: My schedule is very much driven by my symptoms. In the beginning in the first few years, I just kept on recycling writing classes. I found a good local teacher and took classes from her for a few years. And that would force me—you pay your money, you get to show your work twice, that would force me to come up with new story ideas or revise something I was working on. I was very unprepared for the reaction to my early work. Everyone was impressed. And I fed off of that because I hadn't developed confidence in my work. I remember my first writing teacher would give us exercises as homework. At the time, I didn't know that you didn't have to do homework for writing classes: you know, here's an exercise that may help you get started but you don't really have to do it. She gave us one that I thought was kind of dumb, so I played around with it, changed the location, changed the characters. And it ended up becoming a five page story. I'd write a page, stop, then as I was falling asleep, something new would come to me. I'd scribble down notes and use it the next day. It went in directions that stunned me, in terms of language and story. That was my first taste at the joy of creation, and I immediately understood why people stick to writing, painting, even if it means living poor: because you access a part of yourself that you didn't know you had . . . and it's wonderful, addictive.

14H: Can you talk a little bit about the discovery process of your characters? How are you discovering who they are, and what they're doing?

MA: One of the things I've discovered is that I'm good at channeling characters once I have a little bit of an idea. With Ivan and Misha, it actually began as an exercise in a writing class: write a page or two in ten minutes, one character trying to convince another character of doing something he or she doesn't want to do. At this point I'd grown more comfortable writing on the spot. After I had gotten over my initial terror of writing, that is. I started using writing exercises to work on stories or to start something new. So there I was, out of the ether or my unconscious, I was writing about someone called Ivan trying to convince his twin, Misha, to buy in on a scheme to buy a whole bunch of telephone booths. And they were from Kiev, in their early 20s, and lived near each other in the East Village. I have a friend in NY who is a playwright and he was always trying to come up with schemes that would make him lots of money so he could stop working and devote himself full-time to writing. A few months earlier I'd heard from a mutual friend that he was investing in telephone booths. And I had Russia on my mind as this mutual friend had been living in Russia, traveling back and forth, telling me stories; both of us are second generation Russian Jews, so Russia had always interested in me. Those are the threads that created Ivan and Misha seemingly out of the blue. Each time I wrote, I just dug deeper into each of them, then into their father and Smith; I would come up with situations and put them in those situations, and literally take notes on what they'd say, and do, and think. Sometimes I wonder if some of this ability comes from having been a therapist. One of the skills is connecting empathically with the person you are talking to. As a therapist you walk a balance between being completely objective and putting yourself in the mind and heart of patients, often people quite different than yourself. In fiction it's sort of the same. In Ivan and Misha, they weren't based on anybody. Some of the energy comes from having lived in the East Village; knowing that setting helped. Ivan wasn't bipolar right away. That came up a few weeks later. I was aware that my name in Russia would be Misha. As a rule, if the narrator in a story is too close to me in any way, I start to diverge. You can do that just by making them physically different, or temperamentally different. Louis is the closest to being inspired by someone. My grandmother's brother-in-law, Louis Mogalefsky. He had this real rakish disposition. He knew how to enjoy life and he was very different than my father. I didn't know him well at all but that sense of him I had sparked the character of Lyov/Louie. But with Smith, I've no idea where he came from.

14H: New York is central to the story. Do you consider NY to be a character? Do you find you start with the setting first, or the characters first?

MA: It's hard to pinpoint which comes first. The character and the setting seem almost fused together when I write. Sometimes I just start off with a line. And that leads to a character. And I find that different settings pull different energies from me. And I like the energy that New York pulls. San Francisco feels too cute for me, although I've written two stories that are partially set here. I've lived in Boston and New York, and so-far they have a stronger pull on me; perhaps the grittiness and edge of those cities when I lived in them. But I can't conceive of writing without a strong sense of place.

14H: Do you keep a writing schedule?

MA: The short answer is no. And that's because of my health. When one has M.E./CFS the symptoms, especially cognitive functioning, fluctuate by the day, hour, even the minute. When I wrote on interactive media projects I was very disciplined about scheduling. Now, the symptoms dictate what I do, so I've spent the years as a fiction writer trying to end runs and what I call "tricks" to get around the symptoms. Although sometimes I write from sheer force of will and lots of caffeine.

I'm in a free write group and that's been a major way that I sustain my writing. It began back in around 2001 with three writers and myself, although the membership has changed over the years. We'd meet every few weeks. I went no matter how sick I was and found the structure, the sixty minutes we had to write, the feedback, the setting, so to speak, enabled me to write about 900 words each time towards any story or novel I was working on. Or to start a new story. Later, I'd collapse.

14H: Please share with us what you're working on.

MA: I'm working at pulling together a novella and stories, currently titled, "Sorrow's Drive." It's mostly done, but the novella needs editing and one story still doesn't feel quite up to snuff for me yet.

The larger project I've been working on is a novel, "Angor Animi." It began about six years ago as a short story, written completely in my freewrite group. I was still editing Ivan and Misha and didn't feel the desire to start revising the new story but at the same time it felt interesting enough to me that I didn't want to let go of it. Quite miraculously, in the freewrite group I began to write in the voice of one of the minor characters in the story, a nine-year-old girl, and over six years all written as 900 word freewrites, it's become the story of six (or maybe seven) characters, each with their own section, a somewhat similar structure to Ivan and Misha.

The big difference is that I haven't tried to make each section a standalone story as I did with the stories in Ivan and Misha. That book actually began as one story with no intention on my part to go past that story. My agent showed my work, which was really only seven or so stories to some editors back in 2002, and one editor at Henry Holt was very taken with the Ivan and Misha tale. He suggested I write spin-off stories, based on the minor characters. I resisted the idea for a year, (which is when I wrote the novella, "Sorrow's Drive") but my agent would tell me how that editor was always asking about my Russian twins. I can't begin to describe how angry and depressing it can be to have editors almost want to buy your book. But when my anger cooled, I decided to give it a try. Finding the opening line to "Barrel of Laughs" – Louie's story – opened the door for me: "I discovered time yesterday." It was a meditation on time by a 75-year-old Russian exile who's suffered a stroke, and from that the character expanded for me and that was quite a lesson and a key to the other stories: if you find the right point of entry, almost any of your characters can grow and develop in surprising and sometimes profound ways.

But back to your question: "Angor Animi" opens in the summer, on Highway One north of Boston at Elsie's Clamshack. A young man, who's gay, studying playwrighting at Salem State College (obsessed with "O'Neill), and from the working class town of Lawrence sees three strangers, two men and a woman, at another table. They appear impossibly glamorous to him and he awkwardly goes over to them and asks if they are movie stars. They're on the way back from one of the north shore beaches to Boston, and they are most certainly not movie stars but they are taken with the young man's question, and amused.
Later in the story – and much to my surprise! – twin children appear, fraternal again, but a boy and a girl, this time. As I switch to a new section dedicated to one of the characters we meet in the opening section, the story moves forward (or backwards) in time.

14H: Do themes emerge that weren't so apparent when you started writing?

MA: I rarely have any idea where my stories will go, so I don't start with a sense of the themes. Often it's after I'm done that it becomes apparent. The one exception, "Who Did What to Whom?" I tried to bring to life one of my friends who died of AIDS. My intention was to bring him to life as he was such a vivid and unusual man. So I knew it was going to somehow involve the last days of his life. I didn't realize the final scene would be his death. But that's pretty much the only story I've written where I had a sense of the ending. Even in that story, most of what happens in it surprised me. The character of Kevin in that story began as a stand in for me – it was the first story I'd ever written.

I hit a dead-end pretty quickly, which was a good lesson to me as a writer that I had to let go of that character being me. I had to think of ways for it to be more complex and dramatic. I came up with the idea that Kevin was young, new to NY from Buffalo and that after a year, Vinnie's weirdness scares him and Kevin drops him. The theme of betrayal gave the story juice for me.

In the Ivan and Misha title story, that notion that Louie doesn't respect Ivan (in Misha's eyes) wasn't there at first. When I was revising, it came to me and added a dimension that made the final version really work for me.

After Ivan and Misha was published and I realized that, in terms of themes, the one that linked all the stories was the varieties of love: love between brothers; between fathers and sons; mothers and sons; between friends; between lovers. They are all in their way love stories. And stories of exile, from countries, from one's place of birth, from families, from oneself. But I don't start off with those ideas in mind.

14H: A lot of the characters you write are gay characters. Do you consider yourself a gay writer?

MA: I think that's a conversation that's been going on for years for gay writers and writers who are identified with any minority perspective, including women writers. I think of myself as a writer who is gay. My one conscious agenda up to now was to create major gay characters without being self-conscience about it, in the way that straight writers (Saul Bellow, Martin Amis, Phillip Roth, etc. etc.) do. They don't think about their characters as heterosexuals. They write about their sex lives and emotional entanglements but it doesn't start out with, 'oh my character is a heterosexual,' I wanted to write with the same kind of freedom. With all writers who are gay, I see them struggling with different strategies. Many writers who are commercially successful manage to thread the needle: they will have characters who are gay, but they tone it down in some way. Have you read Michael Cunningham's The Hours? I think it was months after I read the book that I realized that all the major characters are gay or bisexual. Clarissa is a middle-aged lesbian living in Chelsea; she has a lover, but from reading the story, it might as well be her roommate. The key relationship in the book is between her and her gay friend who's dying so it's a male/female dynamic being explored, and Virginia Woolf is bisexual, whatever exactly that means in her particular case, and the suburban mom has a bisexual inclination. She is dealing with an attraction to a female friend, but she's a married woman with a kid, and that's what her story's about. As far as sexuality, it doesn't really challenge the reader. I loved The Hours so I'm not criticizing it but rather analyzing how a novel with so many gay characters managed to be a bestseller. For me, I want to create gay characters who have full emotional and sexual lives, but the story isn't about them being gay. Other writers focus on the gay audience, that's who they want to reach, and they tell wonderful stories that rarely find a readership outside the LGBT community. That's not a failure, unless you measure success solely in terms of sales. But it's harder to get published if you're perceived as a "gay" author. Publishing is changing so fast, though, so I hesitate to make that pronouncement about the future. My advice is to write the tales you have in you, the ones that make you feel the time you spend writing is the best part of your life, you wouldn't have it any other way, but to be realistic about the publishing world.

14H: How much are you taking your audience into consideration when you're writing?

MA: I do not at all think about my audience as I write. Other than that, I'm not trying to be an experimental writer so I want the reader to be able to comprehend what I'm doing. When I'm writing I'm completely immersed in the characters and the story, other than wanting it to be coherent and have emotional power. I do assume I'm writing for a literate audience but not one defined narrowly by that word. My 85-year old Aunt in Brighton Beach insisted on reading Ivan and Misha when she'd heard I'm been sending my work to a cousin. I thought it might just kill her. But despite a hard-knocks life (or maybe because of it) and a high school education, she really enjoyed it and lives on. I would hate it if my stories bored people or left then indifferent. I'd feel I'd done something wrong. Still, I still feel the sting of an editor at a leading independent press say my characters never really came to life. It's easier to hear that they simply don't think they can make money on your book.

14H: Please discuss what it's like to write taboo subjects. How are you able to not worry about your audience?

MA: Hmmm . . . I don't want to give anything away to folks who haven't read the book but there is a scene that people find very provocative, even disturbing. In fact, when I realized the book was going there I freaked out! I stopped working on it for months hoping something different would come to me. It was a story I was taking to the Napa Valley Summer Writing Conference to workshop with Michael Cunningham. I was running out of time to submit the full version of it (they'd seen the first half for me to get in), and with barely a few weeks left I decided to go for it and write it to the best of my ability, to keep it real but not tacky or sensationalistic. And for it to make sense in the story, to feel somehow given in the story, and most importantly given the particularities of those characters, that it was inevitable.

To be honest, when the workshop began I was terrified. The first day Cunningham said he found almost all of our work lacking in what it would take to get published. That terrified everyone but after that dramatic beginning he developed exercises for us to do to illustrate what needs to be in the first paragraph to get anyone, especially an agent or editor, to read past one paragraph. Still, there didn't seem to be much hope that my story wasn't one of the ones that bored him. (It most definitely did not bore him, but that took four days to find out.)

But I'm stubborn about my writing and I won't change an element unless I can see for myself why exactly it needs changing from my own perspective. Otherwise, I stick with my instincts, and I've learned to trust them.

14H: There are tributes to other Russian writers, you mention Chekhov. How do those dead Russians influence your writing?

MA: Some of those Russians I mention, I haven't read. Others, such as Dostoevsky and Tolstoy I read years ago. I think what it's more about is that I'm second generation Russian/Jewish, and two generations out, one often still feels a closeness to where your ancestors come from; there's a special certain kind of affinity to that culture: the politics, art, and history of Russia, the Soviet Union, Ukraine draws my interest, in the way, perhaps, someone from a Chinese background will pay attention to Chinese current events, art, history, with that kind of affinity. I only began to read Chekhov when I was well into writing Ivan and Misha, but I was from the beginning curious about him as a cultural icon in Russia. An essay by Janet Malcolm I read in the New Yorker alerted me to that aspect of how Russians think (or thought) about him.

I also gave a lot of thought to which writers Louie would have read. And being a man serious about his native country and its culture, I felt he'd have strong opinions about them. This is also an example of how setting can help develop a character. A Russian intellectual in exile opens a door to what goes on in his inner life, what he'd lived through and how he remembered what he'd lived through, which was most of the 20th century in Russia.

14H: How does the novella differ from your other work?

MA: I've been rereading it. I find it very hard to go back to something I wrote ten years ago. There's a rhythm to it that's different than my other work and it's an effort to enter it again. I've been pulling excerpts from it, which I find hard, and a friend with a great eye helped me a lot with that. But it's also a piece very much based on setting and character: a retired history professor in San Francisco (who is gay) receives a summons to deal with his dead brother's affairs in Boston. The main character, Samuel, is very much a product of Irish-Catholic Boston, and in particular, the Charlestown neighborhood. He's a star baseball player in high school and that gets him entry into Boston Latin and later a baseball scholarship to Harvard. So he's in exile from his family and powerfully strong roots in Charlestown on many levels.

In terms of the new novel, Angor Animi, I'm more confident. I have a better sense of faith that even if I don't know where it's all going, I'll figure it out. I can handle being baffled and confused. And I think that's one of the most important skills to have as a writer. Even if you plot stuff out, there are points where you feel you've lost your way and want "out" from the project. There were several points in writing Ivan and Misha when I told friends I wanted to drive a stake through the heart of my Russian twins and end my agony. You reach a point where you're too committed to let go but not yet convinced you'll find your way to pull it all together into a book you'll be proud of.

14H: So how do you know when it's finished?

MA: For a novel, I don't know yet! This is new. For previous work on long short stories, what usually happens is that about 2/3's of the way through, the ending comes to me. The end of Ivan and Misha, with Ivan showing up in the pickup truck with its unexpected contents throwing pebbles at Misha's bedroom window on their birthday, that came to me out of nowhere, I was falling asleep. I saw it and scribbled the notion down in the notebook I keep by my bed. That clear sense of the ending gave me something to work towards.

For "Whirling Dervish," the last scene came to me long before I was ready to get there.

Where you're writing a book of linked stories, so much of my focus is on each story, that I'm not really paying attention to the whole experience for the reader. Just because I want to get a good story in the end. But I learned that even if it's a good story, it may hurt the experience for the reader. That was really instructive for me. At the last minute I cut two stories out of the book involving a half-brother for the twins about whom they had no idea nor did Louie.

Just a word about the winning awards: It's cliché to say that you win an award and you're happy for four days, and then you go back to your often frustrating, quotidian life. But writers don't get many chances for recognition for their damn wonderful, but hard work. Few earn any money, most can't even get published beyond a story here or there. So I must say that when I won the Northern California Book Award, the recognition from your peers is awesome and wonderful. Maybe even more so for the Gina Berriault Award as it came as such a shock, there was no lead-up to it. Just a phone call from Peter Orner.

14H: If you could give one nugget of advice to aspiring, young writers, what would it be?

MA: If space allows I'll give two, one short and the other a bit longer.

Your opening paragraph is a seduction. When I read a lot of interviews about writing, there seems to be too much of a focus on the idea that the first line needs to be a killer first line. But really all it needs do is to seduce you, the reader. It can be a very quiet first line. But it makes you want to read the second line and the third line. I'll read something with a killer first line but often the work that follows doesn't live up to what's been promised in that first line.

It's commonplace to say that writers should keep reading. That's how you learn. And that's quite true. I believe I've been influenced by every writer I've read over many years, even writers I can't stand now! But look for writers who stimulate the writing/language/story part of your brain. There may not be many. When I first began to write short stories, I hadn't been a reader of short stories. I thought I didn't like them. They're too boring, I'd thought. But I figured if you're going to write one then one should read them. As luck would have it, I discovered William Trevor, then Alice Munro, then Laurie Moore. That was in the mid-90s. Later John Cheever. Their stories changed my life. I found that as I read ideas, words, images, characters came to me. Not that I copied their style or their content, per se, but they spoke to me and woke up that part of my brain from which my writing comes from. So, find those writers that wake you up. Recently I discovered Gina Berriault and she's that kind of writer, too. She writes with precision, with intelligence, with passion, and great beauty. And a profound commitment to deep understanding of her characters that can't be captured in a simple summary. I'd be hard put to outline a typical plot from her writing, but the sense of her characters, the almost magical transitions in the stories make me shiver. There's a quote I remember from an Edmund White essay on Nabokov. Nabokov was asked if he wanted readers coming away from his stories "thinking." If I remember correctly, his answer was "No. I want them to come away shivering."

Left on Monsignor O'Brien

Michael Alenyikov

An excerpt from the novella, "Sorrow's Drive"

Storrow Drive ended in a confusion of signs. One read: *If You Lived Here You'd be Home.* To its right rose grimy white apartment towers: sorry grave markers they might as well be. It was the West End once; Samuel'd read of its demise back when he still made the effort to read the *Globe* to keep up on home, to follow each August's swoon by the Sox; the gossip of politics; the accounts of who'd died. Bits of news for conversation with Peter and Ma via letters and the occasional phone call. But the *rawness* of seeing the West End gone, the rawness of it; the East End alone now, he knew, stranded across the harbor on the far side of the Callahan. Samuel admired an East End true to its past, reminding the world—which, he knew, didn't give a good God damn anymore—that, once, east and west were two; like brothers, one could say. One could, thought the brother who still lived.

Samuel and his Subaru (dusty, grimy, and insect splattered after the journey from San Francisco) arrived none too gently at a crisscross of streets and signs, a buzz saw it felt to him. A din of ratcheting sounds. This town will have its revenge on you; and *better late than never* they screamed to the elderly prodigal, better late than never signaled the flash and blur of traffic lights, headlights, streetlights. I'm not ready, he thought, not ready, not ready, the thought refrained as if the city would take pity if he acted the part of a frightened child.

A long red light allowed him to gather his wits. Then a trusting to instinct guided him through streets that seemed not to have changed in fifty years he'd been away, though their names had been erased, rubbed clean from wherever it was they had set up camp in Samuel's memory, and the buildings that lined the streets were new and old, old and new, no pattern to the urban madness. He had no use for what he's offered: Government Center, Downtown, Faneuil Hall, Callahan tunnel, Logan airport—and what a laugh: the way to the *Freedom Trail.* That passes through home's turf, and he laughed out loud at the idea that the irony was intended for his amusement. Had there ever been a sign that pointed to Charlestown? Wasn't that the point? His heart pounded in the glare of lights. Can a person die of panic? But there—yes!—it's a left on Monsignor O'Brien, he recalled with a rush of blood to his head. A sense of direction he still had. And over the river he drove to find a Charlestown Avenue familiarly dingy and neglected. Over the river? He'd forgotten that home was on the Charles' north side, apart from the city itself. It had migrated in memory as if by small quakes. Oh how they'd thought themselves the *heart* of Boston, the bloody pumping heart and soul of the old town. So many fist fights to prove it.

Over the river, then it's a right for sure. How quickly he found his way in a maze of narrow streets. And there, rising to its modest crest, Charlestown's crown jewel, Bunker Hill. No Beacon Hill for sure, though now he saw homes spruced up: sand-blasted bricks; clapboard hard- scrubbed and painted, hands hired by yuppies, but still a ghetto. The word brought a smile to Samuel. Not once had he ever thought it so and proud he was for seeing it clear this *ghetto*.

He turned from Warren onto School, past Sheafe where School transmigrated into Mystic. Two houses beyond the church (still standing, sprightlier than in memory). And there it is: the old house still there. He double-parked in front, pulled back on the hand brake and looked up.

So small . . . So small it was.

Samuel sat in his car and stared at the house in which he'd been born. Three floors, three flats. They'd had the top and access to the roof, hot tar in summer. And Peter's last address—before the nursing home —was only just down the street. He'd stop there next. Was the cemetery from colonial days still there, with its jagged row of tombstones that tilted one way and the other? Surely they've not razed it! It had looked to him once like an old man's mouth, but now it was a child's proud grin of new grown teeth he imagined. Is it that we see what we want to see? Or is it all changing like the weather in New England and determined as much by the sausage we had for breakfast or the rise and fall of blood sugar from a jelly donut, the flapping of a butterfly's wings in China?

No, it came to him: he did not want to see the cemetery. He did not want to see the flat where Petey'd lived when he'd faced those long years alone. Petey, the brother he'd lost touch with, *let slip away*, let die alone. Petey, the sort that needed family, its sounds, its comforts and irritations; its dailiness. Poor Peter. He'd never wandered far. It was a tough Irish neighborhood and proud they all were of its separateness. Samuel's tongue played with the word—*ghetto*. An oddity of history that tickled his fancy: how an Italian word forced on Jews can hold a collection of poor Irish in the New World. He took out a pint of Dewar's he'd saved over a continent's drive for just the right moment and permitted himself two swallows.

Rain began to fall. Slowly. Large drops of it. How long had he been sitting here? He shook his head to wake his wits. Now a red-haired woman with a child in each hand rushed out the door of his old home, then stopped and looked to the sky, in anger, before darting down the street. "Hurry," she shouted, hands empty of an umbrella, the weather no surprise at all, except to Samuel, too long in the west. Once all life revolved around this square mile. History, now. But Peter had stayed, through two lost marriages. Bedrock to him, Samuel supposed.

Samuel watched the patch of red make its way down the street and disappear around a corner.

The surprise of weather. What was this outrage? When did clouds sneak into a murky night sky? Samuel felt aggrieved, for no worthy reason he can identify. It was only rain, after all.

Swish, swish, the wipers turned on again. How dare the weather interfere with his view of home! But then, on impulse, he opened the car door. A smell so fresh, seasoned with a touch of sea and salt, rushed in. And in a moment he's out and standing. He had no umbrella, no raincoat. A baseball cap he wore. Shame on you, Sammy, his mother's spirit—if it had chosen to haunt this street, to stay close to home—would scold. But his senses were alive to weather, not ghosts and spirits; so Samuel, head up, necked stretched, mouth open, stood swallowing what to him were heaven's tears. The rain fell faster now and Samuel in shirtsleeves grew soaked to the skin. A wind gusted and stole the cap from his head quicker than his reaching hand and twirled it a time or two then plopped it into a rain-filled gutter.

Where was the red-haired woman? And where are all the people he once knew? He swallowed more Dewar's. How wise he was to know it would be needed. *Come back, he implored her, and we will dance.* Samuel's rain-slicked head swells with joy. Come back and I will dance with you and, yes, meet my Da, my Ma, my brother, Pete. Join us, sweet lass.

But the locals had sense enough to stay in when such weather strikes. A loose top to a garbage can was sent banging down the street by the wind. "Can you no longer recognize a Nor'easter?" the well-bred voice awoke in him scornfully; that damn homunculus who'd taken residence in his mind for days and days. "The ocean, I fear, has moved to the other side of your brain. The Pacific's your reference now." Piss off, Samuel thought. But rain is rain and Samuel now recalled the routine, retreating into his car—a kind of home it's been—to consider a hot meal as the sensible what next.

Yet he sat, hands resting on the steering wheel, eyes fixed on the two small windows of the top flat, the clapboard, grayed by years of soiled air, now growing darker, stained by rain, forming fingers like the shadows of stalactites in a cave.

He thought: I am winding down.

Samuel stared at the two top-floor windows and they stared back, dark beady eyes, suspicious of strangers . . . and stranger he was. Piss off, their message. Piss off to strangers in the eyes of all he grew up with.

He'd fled five decades ago. And presumptuous it was to expect a glad-to-see-ya shake, a slap on the back, a hearty embrace.

So small, the windows, so much smaller than in memory. And where were the steps? Five and a small landing he'd carried in memory; but before him the house was near-flush to the street; two steps that were hardly deserving the name, cracked and chipped; and where was the landing he remembered sitting on with Pete and Mickie those long summer nights, their words about Sammy's feats on the mound hurling baseballs as if they were their own.

Charlestown Sammy he was in the neighborhood . . . and at Boston Latin the name stuck; the stare he'd perfected on the mound silenced any who mocked.

Samuel sat in the darkness, aggrieved again at the rain, the wind, the swish, swish of the blades, the surprise of weather.

A knock on the window to his left. Outside the car, a face, but no features. A glance up at the rear view mirror: a startled old man who's seen a ghost looked back. The window was rain-wet on the outside, fogged on the inside. Samuel of the once-nimble fingers searched for the knob to roll the window down, cursed himself at the second knock, remembered it's electric; the soft whir as the window opened, like a man's final exhalation, he thought; and the face: freckled, pale, pink, the red-headed woman close to him, breath a sour smell.

"You lost or something?" she said. "Are you from around here?" He'd expected his mother's voice, faint from hunger as he was. What had he eaten all day? Chinese, too many miles back; later a muffin, blueberry, crumbly at Dunkin Donuts—no, it was a cardboardy bran, fitting for an old man, he'd thought. "Mister, are you okay?" But this woman's voice is raspy, the words hard to discern; why is she speaking so fast, he thought, and felt again aggrieved, then: it's the townie accent, playing musical chairs with their 'r's'. Oh, how hard he'd worked to lose it at Harvard and then in California.

"You looking for someone?" she said, talking slower now as if to an idiot child, and he forgave her raspy voice, which wasn't his mother's—smooth as syrup she'd spoken—aspirations to something higher, better, his father accused when he'd passed the fourth bottle of beer.

"Mister, you've been sitting here for all of an hour. If you're not looking for someone, maybe you'd best go home." A touch of threat now added.

"Who lives up there in the third-floor flat?"

"Me and my kids and my husband, who's a cop and will be home any minute, if you must know."

"I used to live there."

Her face grew blank. "Well, isn't that nice." Her accent thickened so Samuel couldn't tell sarcasm or if it's just the way the young talk to the old.

She's pretty, he noticed. In a weary sort of way. Shadows under her eyes, the color of which he can't make out in the dark, but he knows are blue; the pale blue of a red-headed Irish girl.

Little Orphan Annie, he thought, and fought back a chuckle. Little Orphan Annie, that's who you look like, he struggled against saying because then her decision on him would land on the word loony.

"Look, mister. . ." she began, but he pressed the button and the window rolled up.

Samuel moved the stick into drive and put the pedal down hard, burning rubber; just like the time he and Peter and Mickie had stolen the Chevy. Fled from the scene, they had, and had not been caught. Ditched the car in some sorry end of Somerville. "You're running away." The words Ma'd hurled at him when he said he was leaving for the west came back to him. "Leave and you don't come back," she said and swore in her first letter she'd never meant.

A few blocks later, he stopped at a light. Just one truth he'd hoped to find in the old neighborhood, but he was hungry for something hot now—beef stew and a beer to chase it; and there's the nursing home to find, hidden away in Dorchester's depths; and a place to stay for the night; he'd forgotten essentials – bedrock: hot food and a bed for the night. Foolish to expect more from life, old man, he thought and let go with a laugh and some gas. He pulled out his pint of Dewar's for another sip and reflected on how the muscles of the mouth and ass grow loose in time—and that, yes, this nugget, this truth, hard-earned, will have to do.

The air was misty now. The wiper blades helpless. Street lamps were on, blurred yellow stars distorted by the glass. A tinge of pink in the light. Samuel drove, crawled his way crab-like through the maze of narrow streets, pulling around cars double parked. He was tired, hungry. A horn blasted. Shrill. A man's head—stuck out the window—inches away, traveling in the opposite direction. A hand motioned. Samuel lowered his window.

"Ya got eyes, old man? Don't ya got eyes?" He stared at Samuel, waiting for an answer. When none was forthcoming—Samuel wanted to say, "I've come home"—the man spat in his direction, then drove off.

Samuel worked to steady his hands. He swallowed and felt the dryness of his mouth. He ran his tongue over parched lips. Samuel turned the corner and pulled into an empty space by a fire hydrant. He inhaled deeply as he was taught in a yoga class. Ten deep breaths. He placed himself in a darkened redwood grove. He looked for his wise inner guardian, as he was taught. Yoga for Seniors. He'd swallowed his pride to go. He evoked the smells and sounds of a redwood forest—pungent, whispery —but there was no inner wise man. He was alone among the giant, ancient trees. They've seen too much to know even where to begin, was what he imagined. I'm as important to them as the snails that scavenge their roots or the moss that covers rocks and tree trunks alike. The dew that forms, he'd like to think, is their pity for him. Just now, he would settle for pity. Too late, he thought: maybe I should have gone back, not quit after three classes. But growing old was bad enough. Don't need to be surrounded by mirrors, he'd thought at the time.

He looked up at another three-floor relic of a building. Same as the one he'd grown up in—but not the same. He stretched to roll down the window on the passenger side. Mickie's house. On Chappie, across from old Doherty Park. First floor flat. Samuel crimsoned. All by himself. Five decades and then some, after the fact, he was blushing. Mortification and lust. Mickie was his first. They'd been a trio, he and Peter and Mickie. Inseparable. Grades one through nine. In school. After school. After church. Even after Samuel'd made it to Boston Latin—*The Academy*, Mr. Rourke, his guidance counselor in junior high, had called it with a bit of a sneer—they stayed best of friends. He'd overheard Ma saying to Aunt Peg, "They've gone and separated the wheat from the chaff," and it had made him proud in a sad sour kind of way that had him trying harder to act with Mickie and Pete as if nothing had changed. But there was more to his missing them than the hours lost in travel to Roxbury, hours lost to serious baseball drills, his long left arm and high leg kick his ticket out. And there was a difference in the way he missed his friend and his brother, strong as he missed the easiness of time spent with both, there was that shade of difference that crept up on him, that had him wishing away a feeling that lacked a name even as it twisted his insides. Always one for naming things was Samuel, the university historian, the scholar of Grant's failed presidency.

His first.

Who's idea had it been? Samuel couldn't remember. What he can remember: the fumbling with belts and zippers. Peeling Mickie's shirt off, the shock of seeing what he'd seen before, seen anew. To feel his body with intention. The dropping of pants. Touching what was a sin. They'd both touched at the same time. On a dare. No one's fault that way. Each on their knees in turn. Who first? It can't matter now, thought Samuel. Surely it can't. But the historian needed to know if Mickie wanted it as bad as he. To pin down that truth.

Where? Not here. In Samuel and Peter's room. Da was at Malone's. Ma out to visit Aunt Peg. The bitter taste. He'd spat it out. And Peter walking in. Accounted for at football practice, he'd been sent home with a fever. How could he stand there and gape?

Framed in the doorway. Staring at them. Green eyes blinking, dumbstruck's the only word that'll do. "He's your cousin in the name of Christ," Petey said, in his eyes, the set of his face, Samuel saw what he'll see again, sometimes real, sometimes imagined—in the face of the cop in the toilets, the night the bar on Polk was raided, strangers on a trolley if he crossed his legs, knee over knee, and in his own face reflected—yer no man at all. How does a stranger's face shape this message? Eyes narrow to a slit, the mouth goes crooked, as if the very sight of you makes them want to puke.

And in Samuel's mouth: the bitter taste takes up residence; and words: "Don't tell. Don't tell." But Peter's gone. He runs. Door slams. The pope and Roosevelt rattle in their frames.

They dressed quickly in silence, and after, Mickie had gone his own way. Samuel steadied his hands, which trembled, still, these many years later.

He held tight to the wheel. He'd never forgotten the craving he'd felt—lust such a poor word; but considered now if it was a kind of love that was there too.

Samuel made a fist and pounded the steering wheel. Softly pummeled it so as not to make a sound.

Rebirth

Darlene Pagán

Every brush stroke, he said, you were just hoping
that they would like it, and would let you live.
—Vann Nath

A soldier whispers into Pol Pot's ear
as he sits for his painting. The painter's
breath stops as he watches the grimace
bloom like an open wound, pull taut
the jaw line, lift the mouth, tighten
the skin around the eyes with one invisible
sweep. The painter works the same line
again and again, watches the tension work
into the leader's uneven hairline
like a poor stitch as the whole face bends
and creases like a fan folding shut. Pol Pot

nods, continues to sit for his portrait, the man
who reduced the population by a quarter
from starvation, overwork, execution.
Here is the mouth, drawn in outline
like a worm that will issue orders
until the end. The painter must
correct flaws enough no one notices,
flourish without flattery, smooth the lines
and folds in the face as they do the tortured
dead to avoid becoming one of them.

One of a few to survive the camp, the painter
dreams of his portraits tipping sideways
on the walls, spilling one feature after another—
a doughy chin sliding, a bloated mouth, eyes
rolling like olives into the blood-soaked earth.

As the features fall, children return to life, some
as they were, some as birds and deer, a few
Sun Bears, one wild water buffalo. Women
crawl down from trees like leopard cats
and cicadas. The men shift in the distance
with the look of tigers. By the time the canvas
glows and only the signature of the artist
sits in the bottom corner, the dead
have gathered in their various shapes.
The painter spears the canvas and, one
by one, they crawl through to the other side.

Bundle, Then Swift the New Year

Ruth Williams

Where they pushed
the drunk girl face down on the hood,
a lip print. I watched her split.

Consequently, I want to write
all manner of tender things. Filigree
the moon with other slights.

But all the children in the streets tonight
have dirty smiles, each mouth, a moon that carries
a second mouth around it.

We couldn't bruise easier. Blood taken
leaves a print: blue, black, then green.
A trace of the hit.

Oh, here comes a mouth to cover it.

Cover Artist's Biography

Marilyn Minter was born in Shreveport, Louisiana and currently lives and works in New York. She has been the subject of numerous solo exhibitions including the San Francisco Museum of Modern Art in 2005, the Center for Contemporary Art, Cincinnati, OH in 2009, La Conservera, Centro de Arte Contemporáneo, Ceutí/Murcia, Spain in 2009, the Museum of Contemporary Art, Cleveland, OH in 2010 and the Deichtorhallen in Hamburg, Germany in 2011. Her video *Green Pink Caviar* was exhibited in the lobby of the MoMA for over a year, and was also shown on digital billboards on Sunset Boulevard in LA, and the Creative Time MTV billboard in Times Square, New York.

Minter's work has been included in numerous group exhibitions in museums all over the world. In 2006, Minter was included in the Whitney Biennial, and in collaboration with Creative Time she installed billboards all over Chelsea in New York City. Most recently, Minter was featured in "Riotous Baroque," an exhibition that originated at the Kunsthaus Zurich and traveled to the Guggenheim Bilbao. A retrospective of Minter's work will open at Contemporary Arts Museum Houston, TX and will travel around the country, ending at the Brooklyn Museum, NY.

Minter is represented by Salon 94, New York and Regen Projects, Los Angeles.

Artists' Biographies

Ann Rhoney, a native of Niagara Falls, New York, is acutely responsive to light and approaches her art not only as a photographer but also with the color sensitivities of a painter. Rhoney's work is appropriately featured in the exhibition, "Faking It: Manipulated Photography Before Photoshop," at the Metropolitan Museum of Art, curated by Mia Fineman. She was a recipient of a fellowship from The American Scandinavian Foundation in 1995, culminating in an exhibition, "Angles on Scandinavia," in 2003, at the Scandinavia House in New York. Rhoney's black and white photographs are often completed by applying oil paint by hand, which allows her artwork to transcend the two-dimensional picture plane. Rhoney's elusive images cannot help but gage the viewer's imagination. With a heightened sense of mystery, Rhoney's tempting photographs invite the viewer to conjure up their own interpretation. A graduate of Cornell University, Rhoney now resides between San Francisco and New York.

Deirdre White received a BFA in painting and drawing from Tyler School of Art in Philadelphia, and an MFA in Studio Art from UC Davis where she was a Chandler Graduate Fellow. While at Davis she studied with Wayne Thiebaud and Squeak Carnwath. She has been an Artist in Residence at Oregon College of Art and Craft, and a Visiting Artist at the University of South Carolina. Her paintings have been exhibited across the country from Pennsylvania, Delaware, Virginia, Florida, and Illinois, to Texas, Oregon and California, as well as Copenhagen, Denmark. A San Francisco native, her parents were part of the Beat Generation's poetry scene in North Beach in the late 1950s, before moving the family to Pennsylvania in the mid-1970s. Raised in both California and Pennsylvania, her paintings are disjointed personal narratives that address themes of loss, exposure, erosion, and the weight of our collective anxieties. She is interested in the concept of nature as a socially constructed place, and in landscape as a metaphor for psychological space. Her work is both a critique of, and love affair with, the American west.

Jennifer O'Keeffe is an artist and teacher living and working in San Francisco. She received a BA in literature from Barnard College and an MFA in photography from California College of the Arts. She has exhibited nationally, and her Conspicuous Mountain project was featured in *T Magazine's* "The Moment" blog. Born in the U.S. to European parents, O'Keeffe reinvestigates distinctly American photographic modes in order to understand them on her own terms, from the omnipresent road trip, epitomized by photographers like Robert Frank, in her Conspicuous Mountain project, during which she lived and traveled in a retrofitted cargo van for a summer, to the American documentary tradition in her ongoing project Stanislaus. While attempting to tell the story of a place in transition, she uses the seductive, descriptive, and questionably authoritative power of photography to explore her own relationship to the truth and the mythology of place.

Silk Dress *Ann Rhoney*

Truck *Ann Rhoney*

Everlasting Kiss *Deirdre White*

Red Cloud *Deirdre White*

Sum of Our Parts *Deirdre White*

County Fair *Jennifer O'Keeffe*

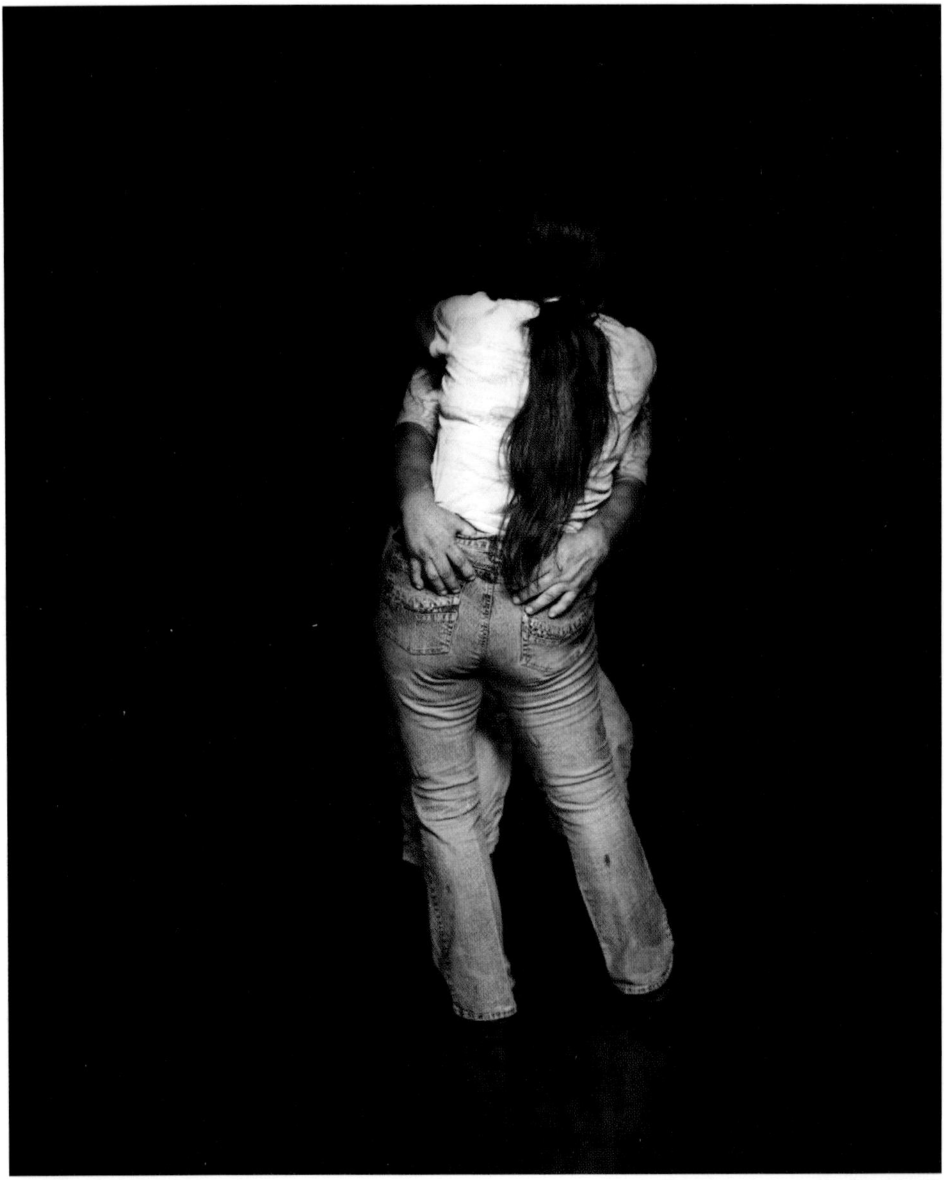

Dancers *Jennifer O'Keeffe*

Hangnail

Heather June Gibbons

If beauty is a place, I want to live there
notating the cries of birds in treble

and fog horns in bass. In beauty,
a mouth tatted shut can still hum.

I worry my foot will wander off
to throb like a beacon or an acid tracer.

The moon is a cuticle—no it's nuclear
a nuclear fingernail clipping. With nothing

left to hide, I zing clean as a cartoon smile.
The teeth are real, the sparkle pure anime.

I slip in and find myself, a stranger.
Slumped in the pew, I fill the holes

of all the vowels with ink. Click-clank:
the roller coaster summons its cars

to a near-vertical incline. Organza no longer
flutters on the clothesline at dusk.

Now the sky itself is a ragged gown
and someone smashed all the china

ground it back down to bone and clay.
Now that speck is a smudge, not a place.

I drag towards it, always, as it recedes—
a constant on the horizon.

Crossing

Heather June Gibbons

I do not name, nor do I whisper after dark.
        In not naming, I call out

in hopes of being called. I am the frame

of a frosted window smeared by hands,
        the window of a night ferry. Dark water moves in me

and passengers stream sternward
        through the gnarls of my hair. I press my face

to the glass, cup my hands to form a seal and all
        reflection is gone. Relief—a darkness

so complete it diminishes water and sky to flatness,
        an absence against which

a few gulls drift backwards.

Assistant

~

Heather June Gibbons

My act requires a certain economy
of gesture, a singe of the blade
in the velocity of white gloves.
Pure metals are too soft. I know

an alloy with no melting point.
I have mastered a calliope of nicks,
my scars so precise they glow
in the spotlight. My assistant purrs

like a torch singer in her sheath
of mauve charmeuse. She pins a bloom
behind her ear and smiles for you
as I strap her to the wheel, snug against

the target: painted outline of her body.
Watch her spangles spark off motes
as the music swells and the wheel spins
and the room spins and my blade

misses, sibilant in the fine hairs of her nape.
Ladies and gentleman, I give you
my beautiful assistant. My first trick.

Anson Mills Fires Its Copywriter

Carol Gore

Retail Products

Welcome to the Anson Mills retail page. You must be here because you have really good taste, or think you do, in grains and everything else. Here you'll find heirloom rice, oats, grits, and polenta available for retail, some varieties that were near extinction before our operation brought them back to life.

Refer to the recipe page for special instructions on how to prepare our grains. Also note that failure to abide by these instructions with exact precision may cause you to feel like a failure, not only in grain cookery, but in life. Add too much moisture or don't cook long enough, and you start to think about all the other instructions you didn't follow exactly right, the minute margins of error you've allowed, and how every tiny miscalculation over the past 38 years has added up and caused the complete derailment of everything you know to be true.

Please, peruse the grains we offer through retail, and happy cooking!

Carolina Gold Rice 14 ounces $6.95, 10 pound bag $69.50

Rice is the ubiquitous ingredient used to prepare a countless number of dishes, and this long grain rice is in a class all by itself. Your hard to please husband will eat this and say it reminds him of his grandmother's cooking, but not nearly as good. His mother will eat this rice you cooked exactly right, or so you thought, and not say anything at all. She'll also rearrange your furniture. You wonder if he can afford to eat this rice anymore without your employee discount and his business ideas that seem great at the time but never go anywhere. And if you ever found out she placed an order here you'd bribe whoever you had to in the warehouse to make sure her order got lost, even the guy with the bowl cut and creepy eyes. You know that guy would do it. No, you hope she never tries ordering this rice at all and he's stuck eating Uncle Ben's, and you sincerely hope it's the precooked kind that comes in the microwaveable bag.

Perfect for risottos and stir-fry.

Rustic Course Polenta 12 ounces $7.50, 10 pound box $75.00

A creamy mouth feel and floral aroma make this polenta the best in the United States. No matter how good it is though, and even though you stood over the stove for hours, stirring constantly, making sure the bottom didn't stick and burn, and you still have the scars from the "polenta napalm," when hot grain would explode from the pot and stick to your hands, arms, face, even after all that he still left you. Maybe you forgot the filtered water, maybe you forgot a lot of things. You forgot to exercise everyday and have a baby. You forgot to quit smoking. He told you smoking was bad for estrogen. Bad estrogen is bad for relationships. Would she cook him this polenta? Would she? Yes, she owns several pieces of lingerie and is young enough to bear children without much intervention, but you doubt she'd ever make this polenta. When she came to your house for dinner that time she'd never heard of kale.

Try it with a tomato ragu. Yum!

Slow Roasted Farro 12 ounces $6.95, 10 pound bag $69.50

Everyone tells you not to have a three way when you're married but then you go and do it anyway. Why? Why did you agree to have her over for dinner and drinks, after he talked about how witty she was, how smart, so fit, and maybe she'd influence you to go to the gym? She came over and you cooked this farro with shrimp and sauteed kale to impress her, or him, and then you drank too much cabernet, or maybe just enough, and it seemed new and fun, and he was right, she was very fit, and he seemed like he really wanted to, and anyway before you knew it, it was happening. First she's blowing in your ear, then she's kissing you, and how could you stop her?

I wouldn't recommend this with shrimp.

Antebellum Course Grits 12 ounces $5.95, 10 pound bag $50.00

Anson Mills course grits have a flavor and texture that can't be matched by other grits on the market today. They're ideal for a special breakfast, like the morning after your first three way. She chewed the grits and eggs with the secretive smile that intrigued you at the time, but you soon learned to suspect because it started to feel like it wasn't for you anymore. After your second three way, she asked where those delicious grits were, not realizing that Anson Mills grits weren't the kind that come in a packet and only require hot water mixed in. These grits require time and careful planning. You aren't very good at planning, especially when an unexpected second three way is thrown at you. After the third three way that you really weren't into but went along with because you didn't want to be a downer, you served the grits in the packet the next morning, thinking she might not notice, but she turned up her nose. He followed her lead and left his plate untouched.

These are the preferred grits of you and your spouse's three way partner.

Handmade Stone Cut Oats 12 ounces $5.95, 10 pound bag $59.50

Filling, healthy, and delicious. You had the forethought last night to start them in the crock pot before bed so they'd be ready for breakfast this morning. You were so excited and proud and even put the one blooming camellia from the yard in a vase, but the blossom fell off when you set it on the table, and that's when he told you. Now you hate camellias. Once, you baked these oats into oatmeal cookies and brought them to the picnic because you thought you all could just be friends, but were they really looking for a bathroom when they were gone for so long? You had to make conversation with her blank husband for close to thirty minutes. Her husband fed one of your cookies to his stupid, slobbering dog while you stared out across the field, waiting for them to reappear. Your face trembled from holding a smile for too long, and began to ache.

These oats are better than grocery store oats.

You should know by now Anson Mills grains are better than other grains so there's no point in saying that in a snappy way right now. Remember, the extensive cooking time may seem like an inconvenience, but it's actually a great way to distract yourself from the fact that you're going to die. With all the trouble it takes to measure, stir, and time, you'll never once think about the novels half-written, or how you've only ever been truly loved by your parents, which is nice, but not enough. Be glad for the distraction, for it will soon end when you sit down to eat with the wilted camellia that reeks of death. Please come back again.

Happy Birthday

Michael Dickman

I don't know you but I want to

tell you something

This morning when the garbage truck passed by

my baby son said *Mama*

Mama!
We are born once
and only once

Everyone is happy about it

The owl I saw
on a telephone poll in Portland
is gone

A small darkness against the larger dark

The days just keep being

Days

Super Ball

Vincent Craig Wright

In front of 7-Eleven, standing there looking at nothing, Ronnie-Ann from Modesto asked did I want to tweak out.

This gold Lincoln with a bondo door tied shut ticked in the sun.

She said her mom was home with her boyfriend the asshole so we had to go in the bathroom.

She smiled at the guy behind the counter, pulled me in and locked the door.

I told her I'd only known a boy Ronnie on my baseball team.

"I looked like a boy until I was twelve," she said and kissed me, pushing the back of my leg against the cold toilet.

She felt me up while I snorted a line.

I stood there seeing sparkles like super balls.

When I was little our neighbor, Wayne Thomas, who said he was police but nobody believed him (Daddy said he collected insurance), cut a super ball in half then went off smoking. I wanted it whole again. I tried to hold it together.

I was snorting another line with this banging at the bathroom door.

Then Ronnie-Ann made out with the thick dude from behind the counter like they were on TV in another room. I thought maybe they couldn't see me until he pushed his glasses up his face and said get the hell out of there.

I did but he'd locked the front door to the store so I went to the cooler and got a Mountain Dew and drank half and put it back and got another. Then stuck a Slim Jim and two Snickers and a pack of Salem 100's for Mom in my pockets.

This woman pulled up outside in a wet mini-van like she'd come from the car wash or some place raining and stood there with her hands between her eyes and the glass like binoculars, pointing at the lock like I was supposed to let her in.

I went and sat on the counter and looked at the cash register but there was nothing but buttons so I took a bite of Slim Jim and spit it toward the trash can and looked at the lady outside then at the bathroom door then back at the lady like she should accept me for who I am right now.

She left like she'd never come back.

The guy came out of the bathroom and told me get the hell out again and I was on my third Mountain Dew with a half-pack of Juicy Fruit in my mouth and when he opened the front door the pay-phone was ringing and I started to answer but didn't have anything to say so I walked home throwing rocks at signs, trying to remember everybody I needed to get even with.

Way before Daddy left, Wayne taught me how to tell a real super ball—hold it straight out and drop it and if it bounces back up as high what you got's "gen-u-wine."

A week after the 7-Eleven shit Ronnie-Ann from Modesto walked up at the mall and said, "We didn't do anything," and offered me a pretzel.

On the escalator she said, "He lets me get beer and I let him kiss me's all."

I kept stepping back down but not as fast as the stairs took us up.

"Yesterday the mall was cracking," she said.

I watched twin boys, like three-years-old and in little sailor outfits, walking with their mom.

"I'm going back to Modesto," she said like I was supposed to say something.

I didn't know what. I was trying to hold back the handrails, going nowhere until the twins came up with their mom and perfectly shaped, purple, shopping bags.

We went out in the parking lot in some bushes by these huge robot-looking air conditioning things and smoked out of her pipe like we weren't anywhere in the world.

I put my head in her lap and listened to the air conditioners and thought about the city band tuning up at the community center across the street when Daddy worked for the telephone company.

She put my hand on her leg and we didn't move at all.

Sometimes I think Wayne was trying to show me how the world's going, get me thinking things scientists and preachers think, looking at both sides and the whole.

Then I think Wayne was this loser who hung out with kids and I don't know if I'd recognize him.

I had a picture of him holding his switchblade in one hand, a cigarette in the other, and his face pushed into the sky blowing smoke rings but you can't find any.

They're too high.

They're gone.

I found the super ball he'd cut in two. The wrinkled tape losing its sticky reminded me of band-aids in the bathtub and when I yanked it off all I had was two pieces, the sparkles just spots.

I thought to send Ronnie-Ann a half one day when I thought I saw her but didn't.

Hood Ghazal

Daniel Donaghy

Philadelphia, PA

In the '90s, slumlords circled like hawks over Kensington,
snatched up the empty row houses in Kensington,

cut them into apartments for transients, spread no heat,
leaking roofs, creeping mold throughout Kensington,

brought alleys clogged with diapers, syringes, rotten meat,
brought crack dealers, squatters, prostitutes to Kensington,

scoured the obits, brought nasturtiums, flowering cat's feet
to grieving widows looking to move quickly from Kensington,

let those houses crumble, bought out neighbors to complete
the transmogrification of entire blocks of Kensington,

left graffiti, junkies, burned-out cars in the streets,
left boarded windows, shuttered stores across Kensington,

which once held block-long textile mills, each with a fleet
of trucks, its own commissary, gangs of workers from Kensington,

where once in every parlor danced a piano, every girl beat
on the porch a rug her father had made for her in Kensington.

Bird in Hand

Philip Belcher

After Shelby Lee Adams' photograph, "Anne with Pigeon, '95"

Of all the photographs of people
with beasts—"Enos Holding Snapping
Turtles, '07," "Jane with Diddles, '94,"

"Shithead the Pony and the Noble Family,
'03"—this print of Anne cupping a pigeon
bites like an ax into pine's soft meat.

This woman has become a tree. Skin as etched
as bark, her face the whorl of a severed
limb scored into silence by the mountain's

taloned weather. In the foreground, the dark
bird stares from the nest of Anne's fingers.
It's as if she wants me to take her prize,

to see what she sees behind
the pigeon's eye, to share the panic
felt through the feathered chest.

Slur

~

Philip Belcher

Ten years have scrubbed most of the fire
from the cinder blocks. The lawn has ceded
its grass to sand, to bottles tossed from cars
on Highway 3. Until today, I've never stopped,

listened to the wind blow through the beans
and the ribs of the double-wide. That night
comes back, and I hear the band at the armory
covering Skynard's *Simple Man.*

I see in shards of glass the sneer of Tanner Bates
drunk on Chivas and lust, stumbling into
Andrew's wife, cupping her breast too long,
Andrew reddening until *faggot* breaks

through the bars of his teeth. And Tanner,
following them home, waiting in his Ford
until the sitter's gone and all the lights are out.
No sound but the pines' soft sweep, like a sheet

sliding over skin. This man, a friend until
three hours ago, lifts a five-gallon can
from the trunk, empties it in one turn
around the trailer, and waits for flames

to tear the dark. I remember the preacher—
tall behind three caskets, singing *His Eye*
Is on the Sparrow louder than anyone else,
and remarking how these parents read

the Bible to their daughter every night,
how when dawn stabbed the smoking lot
and the firemen twisted their hoses closed
a page of Leviticus washed to the street.

Cockroach

Daniel Riddle Rodriguez

1.
These are things that happened before we were together. The kinds of things you'd keep after, pressing me in that roundabout, hat-in-my-hand way of yours. Doesn't it feel, I don't know, unnatural to me? You projected such indifference I knew our whole relationship was like that: a projection. An act. Like the first night I followed you into your apartment, and you were so nervous you dropped your keys in the hallway. You smiled like *aw shucks* before bending down to scoop them up, spinning them on your fingers like some sort of cowboy. American boy. Gunslinger. I bet you really thought you shot me down, like your bullet had my name on it.

2.
No one ever says *I want to be a cockroach.* It's an LA thing. You just wake up one morning a cockroach.

It went like this: little girl, big dream, bus ticket. I liked the window seat. I pressed my face against the glass, giving testimony to every long shadow on the landscape. I kept a ragged map in my pocket. I wrote my name in the bathroom of each truck stop between home and California. My fingers smelled like felt markers.

You told me that was poetic. You daisy-chained metaphors, odes to what you called my *lovely nuances,* and read them aloud to friends. You the poet, me the budding actress. But only a background actor, really: a cockroach.

You held me close then and I felt your breath. You stroked the tattoo on my shoulder. The cockroaches will outlast us all, you said. As if poetry could fix anything.

3.
I stayed in an apartment above a bar. I had no car, no phone—only a canvas bag of slugs for the payphone downstairs, a few loose singles to

bum rides to casting calls. My roommate called herself Valentine, said it was her *for real* real name, but she was a cockroach, too, so she was probably lying. Her story was similar to mine: girl, dream, ticket. Except she'd landed a couple of speaking parts, some line work to rehearse while the rest of us pretended to eat our Cobb salads and hoped for a SAG card.

Valentine had a muscle car, an old Mustang the color of mayonnaise, eggshell interior. We rode around together—picnics in Culver City, bottles of burgundy in the trunk. She wore poom poom shorts and cat eye frames. I wore an ascot and made faces in the rear view: sultry lips, pouty lips, all the lips in my bag. I pretended I was Holly Golightly, or Audrey Hepburn, really, and if not Audrey herself, someone who looked okay standing behind her. Just another pretty roach on 57th and 5th, the Tiffany's storefront window.

We drove fast and made believe the world was smaller than it was. Like we could fit it all behind us. We were fueled by something, an ancient thing that charged our angst.

Valentine said it was the red wine. She said it was poverty.

She had other friends, too: women who smoked Newports to the filter and stuffed their ankles into pale blue Crocs; dancers squirreling money away and never making any pretense about night school, finals week; women whose indifference was earned, worn like a second skin, and not just a projection.

And this was the essence of us; we were poor and we knew it.

4.

One morning, Valentine smashed the ceramic cookie jar we kept over the fridge. Mostly copper coins, some silver. I was at the kitchen table, harvesting marshmallows from my cereal.

Alright friend, she said. Tough love time. We're out of cash and favies and parties to ask them from. But we're young and we're beautiful in the youngest, most beautiful town in the world.

Valentine called it our silver lining, the fact we were born women.

It does more than move velvet ropes, she said. Our silver lining makes magic happen. Valentine lit a cigarette and spread our bills out on the table. Past due. Remit soon. She said; Want to make these disappear?

Every day for ten days Valentine taught me her disappearing act. We shoved her box spring into the corner to make space for the brass pole. Her room was a makeshift stage. Bottles of bronzer on her vanity, bottles of dye.

She taught me how to climb the pole, how to invert myself. There were names for the things she taught me, animals mostly: the Firefly Spin, the Bee's Knees. Remember, she said, the pole is a prop, not a dance partner. It's like one big dildo all the little dildos fuck you with by proxy.

The little dildos? I said.

All the guys in the room, silly, she said. Just keep your snatch on the brass and you'll be fine.

So everyday for ten days I kept my snatch on the brass.

I told myself I was fine.

5.

I told you about my first night. The club was full—peopled with silhouettes in trucker hats, mustachioed men—a hither and thither scatter of bravado and loose bills. It felt like hell would feel. Like some wobble bass purgatory, every lost soul waiting for deliverance—or really just a blowjob, a mound of hair to lock their teeth onto. I locked myself in the bathroom stall and lifted my feet up, thinking: I want to make these disappear.

Valentine found me in the stall, but I doubt she had to look hard. She came prepared. I held the martini glass while she crushed two pills into powder and sprinkled it over the drink like some kind of garnish. Abracadabra, she said, whisking me away. I want you to meet someone.

He was a regular. An old man. Pockmarks on his face, dreadlocks like a portion of spaghetti on his head. He had gold fronts and every dollar he pressed against me put my skin into quarantine—or maybe something less tangible, even, like my soul.

He smelled like lavender tonic.

He smelled like pomade.

He smelled like wildness distilled into tiny bottles and sold in all those ethnic storefronts you see out the transit bus window. Did you never see them, poet? Those times you stared out the glass like there was something only you could see. Weren't you ever really looking? The wild things all around us.

We found a private booth.

I wore the man's money on my hips.

I traced his pockmarks with my fingers and when he climbed on top of me it seemed like Mother Nature herself were vindicated.

My second skin earned.

I told you these things and you cried in that way people cry when other people are watching.

6.

There are times people ask me about me. I smile and tell them about cockroaches. I tell them they cannot be drowned, frozen or starved. That they sense danger. I tell them they weren't put here to outlast everything—God didn't make apples just to drop them on your head, after all—but they will.

It's like that time we signed you up for that open mic downtown. And you were mad because you had to follow the feminist poet—a pixie-cut barista, her notebook dense with girl power. (Sapphic ballbusters, you called them.) There was a tattered couch in the corner, Turkish grounds on the floor. I sat next to a guy with a hobo bag and a lapdog. While you were reading, he leaned in and whispered in my ear. He's talking about you, right?

Not me, I said, taking his Papillion into my arms. Just my nuances.

Your nuances?

Only the lovely ones.

We pet his lapdog together while you compared my loveliness to a summer's day, a springtime shrub. Her loveliness is a springtime shrub, you said.

The Papillion licked my fingers. Its owner asked me who my favorite president was.

All the dead ones, I said.

We locked ourselves in a bathroom stall. His dog, perched on the toilet tank, watched us. The man didn't speak. He tore at my skirt. He hanged my panties on the coat hook.

When it was over I watched him zip up, hock phlegm onto the tile.

Did you know some roaches mate for life? I told him, lighting a cigarette. They just stay pregnant forever. Did you know that?

If the man knew, he didn't say, just gathered the Papillion in his arms, pressed a bill into my hand, and left.

I sat on the toilet bowl and held my feet in the air.

I heard the sound of snapping fingers and knew you were waiting for me.

I closed my eyes and imagined I could wait there forever. I would sit and molt until my dead skin formed piles around me, until the piles grew so large the world would be tiny in comparison, infinitesimal. I would take the world then and leash it, and it would put up such little resistance it could hardly be said to have resisted at all. The world would finally know who owned it. It would know all about it.

I opened my eyes and flushed the cigarette down the toilet.

I put my panties in my purse and went back out to you.

I was fine.

Obituary

Molly Faerber

You are born in a post-and-beam house where now four pear trees hug the east wall, one each for you and your brothers. Basil spilling from window boxes, the well your father covered once you learned to walk. It had not occurred to him before, then suddenly there was you, a daughter—the leaf that fell of its own accord as he stood in the yard on the day of your birth. The sky pink, the world sharpening, brightening. You, born on the first day of summer.

You in a striped swimsuit, your body a birch tree, a branch—so young then. Arc of your dive into the sea, of the scar on your bicep. Committed to my tongue like the shape of your name, a stirring of wings behind the teeth. Your childhood garden full of starlings and wrens. You in a forest in Brittany, birdcalls blossoming into your empty hand. You lay a finger to my lips, *écoute*. Your mother teaching you Latin, your brothers leaving one by one.

You at fifteen before we have met, your face taking shape. The sharpness of you, all your edges held tensed. You laughing or screaming or singing with your mouth wide open, surrounded by boys. Fifteen, and you have barely touched anyone. One of them saying, *please*, and you considering it, briefly, because he had said please. At the seashore, running, you wing yourself into open space. Walking up the embankment without your coat. Your bitten nails.

You are given a camera at Christmas, you without any inclination to document your own face. You jumping the gates at Barbès, staring at strangers in the opposite seats until they notice. You—*I've lost my ticket*—and they, believing. You duck your head, sheepish. You, a child, saying your brothers have all died. The lie going sour in your stomach later, your friends having already forgotten. Especially in America, you give men who do not interest you a name not your own.

You reciting the inventory of your names to a girl with long, straight hair on the first night you live alone. Every day, you walk up the rue Saint Jacques, rue Racine, avoid the rue Mouffetard. You walking home carrying bread. Pensive outside the door of that long-haired girl, falling in love. You cannot stop thinking of that hair. It slides like water on your skin when she—but you don't tell me this. In among your things, four rolls of film of only her. Your teeth, when we do meet, an interruptive dashed someplace I can cover with a scarf. You say she was a dancer and ate very little. You who are perpetually peeling fruit, your desire for sweetness in all its forms.

You stepping from a plane in New Mexico where you know not a single person. This place, the farthest you could go. You learn to pound stakes into the ground, to drive a car, to build a fire. To be with men, their names irrelevant. You barefoot in the earth, dust coating your calves and your hair grown too long. Your weekly phone calls, your father on the other end. He has begun to ask in his perfect English when you will be home. Your name so very different in these people's mouths. How it sounds when shrouded in the voice of the long-haired girl. In order to appease your mother you ask people to take pictures of you in various places. You, suntanned. Your craving for salt.

Your Paris apartment where every surface holds an open novel, and you fall first into one and then the next. You in an unmade bed, reading for days. Not realizing you would have to find your way back into a native tongue. You capturing with an expensive lens the faces of those you see in the street. Their expressions unknowingly observed filling boxes beneath your coffee table. You in the school courtyard, fingering a book, smoking absently. The first word you ever say, you exceptionally young. Your examinations—how you surpass two brothers but not the third, your parents' pride. That oldest brother who still calls you little sister, baby girl. He is an interpreter now—you look nothing alike.

You and I, after we have met on the rue Saint Marc—you with an armful of flowers, me asking who they are for. You—*just for me*. We two picking tomatoes from your mother's yard in the country. Pear trees in bloom, yours that climbs highest on the side of the house. You—*taste this*, me not caring for tomatoes, my lips parting regardless. You watching women who step from cars on the rue Saint Honoré when you have barely touched anyone. You calling me selfish months later, having always been a good judge of character. In the garden then, you not belonging to anyone. Basil leaves clinging to wet fingers. Your abortion in Santa Fe, that English boy with the sweet voice and the dog like a small gray wolf. You turn to kiss me like none of it had meant a thing. You—*it was a beautiful dog*. You and that dog in the desert, howling at the sky. The boy on his back under the stars; the precise fingers of the long-haired girl; my mouth poised above the slickness of skin.

You leaving for London and me for New York—leaving you. You leaving me, not quite a death. You driving through the countryside with a succession of other people, a list of names I learn from friends. You speaking before a crowd. Not so beautiful anymore as when I knew you—it seems to happen with impossible speed, your face suddenly changed. Your thinness, a sickening even then, and you so young. Willfully unaware on the train north. The comfort of a place you have never been, how an unfamiliar town consoles. Your first few days in England when you call me too early, I just waking, forgetting not to say as I put down the phone, *I love you*. You on the underground, in buses, you sometimes in taxis where the driver cannot guess from your accent the place of your birth. That coast so green, and you among apple trees. Barefoot in the ruins of a church, telling me to take off my shoes. Telling me to take off my dress. Your hands full of daffodils as you wait on a corner for the light to change. Truth souring in your stomach. You laying out photographs of the desert and the seaside, of streets you can still name in Paris and Camden and Santa Fe, a hundred other places. Your pictures distributed among us when you are dead.

You making me stand in the blue stream of light from a stained glass window in a church by the river, how cold it was between those wet stone walls. You naming flowers, small stars of hydrangea speckling your jacket where I shook them out. You laughing with your mouth wide open. Your father having died already, just the year before. The books he leaves you filling makeshift shelves. The bruises you leave on both of my wrists. Walking home through the park at four-thirty in the morning, not scared at all. Leaving your camera with me, just to be safe. You asleep in a photograph I take, trapped and waiting like a ghost inside the canister for months. In London you finally discover and send it to me in my upstate valley beset by snow. You living out a year by one river, me by another. Your hands slicing tomatoes. Held now between the pages of a novel, your face unknowing—you.

Tyosha

Jane Rose Porter

Brooklyn, New York, 1978

The rain came down so hard, the droplets leapt from the pavement. It did not stop him. Yurik leaned into the storm as he walked. Trees thrashed, traffic lights bled, the sun—a far off patch of light diffused against the rain. The stoplight turned green and horns screamed at him to get a move on, but Yurik took his time crossing the seven lanes of traffic.

He knew he was in trouble, not just with God, but more importantly, with his manager at work. He should have been at the synagogue hours ago to clean the toilets and straighten the prayer books, to ready the place before the morning service. But it was his wife's birthday—occasion enough, he'd decided, to skip one scrub-down of the House of God.

His pajamas clung to his chest and thighs. Yurik was soaked but relieved to be alone. When he'd started his walk that morning, the Brooklyn boulevard brimmed with every stage of life: mothers pushing strollers, children running ahead of them, teenagers in roller skates, at least one or two old men doing arm aerobics on a shaded bench. But heaviness had hung all around as if to smother the light and once the first droplets fell, the sun recoiled, the sky sheeted rain, and the street emptied. A few people stood under awnings, waiting out the storm, otherwise, the street belonged to him.

His wife turned 25 today. Yurik tried to imagine what she might want for her birthday. A mop? Chocolate? He'd always been terrible at these things. He could have asked Mama that morning before he left the apartment, but he did not want to start his day by talking to her.

He called her *Mama*, but she wasn't his mother, and he didn't like her much. Liking each other hadn't been part of the arrangement when Yurik Milner and Vera Robinov decided they would leave Leningrad and move together to Brooklyn. She cooked his meals, changed his baby's diapers, slept on the pullout sofa in the living room. Everyone assumed they were mother and son, though he knew of ugly whispers among the Russian émigrés on the Ocean Parkway benches. *Let them talk*, Vera would say. He was married to her daughter. Calling her Mama wasn't such a stretch.

A group of old women huddled under the canopy of a corner store, wrapping each other's hair in plastic bags. He shouldered past them and went inside.

Tinkling bells. Colors piled atop each other. The shelves overflowed with foil, shrink wrap, aerosol cans, kitty litter sacks; the narrow aisles stacked with unpacked inventory boxes: toilet paper, Jell-O, Frito Lay bags poking from splayed cardboard flaps. A wall of Hostess: Sno-Balls, Cup Cakes, Twinkies, Double Tender Finer Donuts. The cashier, a frail old woman in a clear bonnet, lifted her pale face from a crossword puzzle to acknowledge him.

Toward the back, Yurik found another room, just as full. StarKist Tuna, pretzel jugs, Flav-R straws in blue and white. Crates of Dr. Pepper, Mountain Dew, Tab. A humming freezer. Morton's Frozen Fish Sticks. Creamsicles. Bright orange Tang jars. Rows of Sloppy Joe cans, SPAM, Heinz Baked Beans. He examined the grains in a sack of rice, counted the slices in a package of white bread, bent a beef jerky stick back and forth between his hands.

His house slippers squished beneath him through a pathway of Windex and Clorox. A bald man with arched white eyebrows grinned at him from the labels of cleaning products. He knew the face from work, had pulled the bottle from the plastic bucket he wheeled down the synagogue halls. *Who the fuck are you laughing at Mr. Clean?* He almost said the words aloud.

"What you looking for?" a man's voice demanded and Yurik darted his eyes across the row of bald-headed faces as though he might find the speaker among them. A heavyset man with a charcoal mustache stood against the far back wall, studying Yurik. He scuffled deeper into the aisle, out of the man's sight. Bright sponges hung along the wall, packages of metal Brillo piled in a big bin, the kind Mama had scrubbed the dishes with that morning, her face contorted with effort, or anger—he could never tell anymore.

He'd left the apartment without saying a word to Mama that morning. He wondered if she remembered Ella's birthday. Of course, she did. She always reminded him of such things— to buy flowers, to wipe the child's mouth, to take the trash to the curb.

He lifted a heart-shaped Whitman's Sampler to his face and sniffed its clawing sweetness. He mouthed the names on candy wrappers: *Laffy Taffy, Pixy Stix, Jujubes.* The sounds of words and how they'd always felt in his mouth changed in English. He'd picked up the habit of practicing his reading wherever he could—examining billboards and store signs and leaflets stuffed into his hand on the street.

"Jimmy, get over here. I need you!" The old woman hollered from behind the register.

The man grunted. "All right Ma," he said. "Hold yer horses." He made his way to the front of the store, turning to Yurik as he passed. "This ain't no museum," he said.

The shelves suddenly shook around Yurik as a train sped by on the track overhead. He used to practice his English on that Q train, getting on at Coney Island, taking it all the way to Queens and back, moving from light to dark to light as the car dipped underground and rose again onto the elevated track. He would glimpse the magazines and books of nearby passengers, sounding out the names of train stops. He remembered that last long ride he took, how he sat in an empty car above ground when the doors opened and a pigeon flew inside. The bird flailed from ceiling to window to floor, searching for some way to break out. It slammed into windows and seats, nicking Yurik's head as he held very still. As they neared the station stop and the train shrieked along the tracks, the pigeon settled on a seat and cocked its head at Yurik. Its face gave off a purple and green sheen—he could remember it even now in that aisle of brightly colored candy. At the next stop, the bird disappeared into a small commotion on the platform and the car filled with silent slumping bodies as though none of it had happened. He'd felt suddenly and acutely alone with all those people in the car and decided he would not take those long rides anymore.

Now he liked the soothing numbness of stores best—their many items, ordered and labeled, aisle-by-aisle, piles and shelves and pyramids of countless crackling colorful things. He could wander in a store for hours, lifting packages, sniffing them, turning them over in his hands, trying to put a taste and touch and scent to each one. Smooth words in Russian sounded harsh in English; sharp words were dulled, their spellings inexplicable: cantaloupe, pretzels, bologna. He had gone from Yurik to George. And there was *Tyosha*: mother-in-law, the most peculiar translation he'd seen yet. He'd first learned the term in the airport when they arrived—three words all strung together, lines connecting them as if to take up as much space as possible.

"Where are you staying?" the officer behind the Plexiglas in customs had asked that afternoon.

Yurik slipped the scrap with the Ocean Parkway address on it under the window slot.

The man studied their passports.

"What's your relation?"

Yurik wondered what it mattered, but decided not to argue now. Things would be different here. "Jew," he said. "My relation, Jew-itch."

As if there was a need to ask. Why else would they be there?

"Re-la-tion," the officer said slower now, nodding at Vera, Yurik shaking his head in regret.

"Who's she?" the man tried, flicking his chin at Vera.

"*Tyosha*," he said, and the man behind the glass narrowed his eyes. Sweat poured from the temples of his ruddy face.

"Mother?" he tried.

"No." Yurik shook his head.

"Wife?"

"Wife mother," Yurik said.

"Mother-in-law?"

A strange phrase.

"My wife mother," he repeated.

"That's mother-in-law, buddy," the officer said, his face expressionless.

Yurik stuffed the chocolate box back on its shelf and mouthed the phrase now as he had then—*mother-in-law, mother-in-law, mother-in-law*—wondering, what did the law have to do with it?

"Where's your wife?" the officer had asked him.

"No wife," Yurik said. "In Russia." And then not knowing the word for it, he pressed his palms together, lay his cheek against his hand and shut his eyes as if to mimic sleep.

Vera leaned toward the Plexiglas then. "Scuse me," she said and cleared her throat, enunciating each word slowly, "She. Iz. Dead."

Yurik studied the toes of his boots as she spoke. They were scuffed, his feet sweating fiercely inside. He hadn't wanted to waste their little luggage space on such a bulky item, but now—those salt stains and the caked-on dirt—how could he come to America in such shameful shoes?

"Can I help you?" The woman's voice came from behind him now, the cashier leaning on her hands over the counter top, blinking her watery eyes at him. Her son stood with his arms crossed behind her, his face a younger, harder version of her own. Yurik shook his head, looked down at his soaked house slippers, his face getting hot. He didn't want to speak to anyone. Not yet. He had woken this morning to the dream of his wife. He had turned on his side and pulled her close to him, pressed his cheek against the wings of her shoulders, kissed the softness of her arms, ran his hands along the curve of her hip, tracing the arc of smooth bone down the length of her thigh and up again. Their breath was perfectly aligned and her smell—a smell like kneaded dough and apples—surrounded him.

Then something crashed outside his door—a pot or pan—and Ella rolled away from him and the bed creaked noisily and the ceiling fan thrummed and a car outside honked its horn and Lucy began, as if on cue, to cry, and his wife was dead again, gone from his bed.

Yurik said nothing to the cashier and made his way to the open cooler against the wall.

Skim milk. Semi-skim. Whole. His lips curled around the sounds in his head, the bottles lined up behind a curtain of thick plastic strips in the refrigerated case—four full rows in plastic, glass, cardboard containers. Ella would not believe how much there was to choose from in this place.

The bells of the door jangled and when he turned his head, the old woman and man had disappeared from the counter.

"Sure I can't help?" She stood beside him, slight, a thinning patch of hair visible beneath her translucent bonnet. She held her bony hands out, the thick lumpy fingers trembling, a network of wormy veins spreading beneath them.

Yurik shook his head again and ducked into another aisle, this one full of grinning toddlers. Disposable diapers. It was time to start using these American diapers—the kind you could wrap into a bundle and toss in the trash. Yet Vera stubbornly insisted her grandchild would not be wrapped in plastic like a loaf of Wonder Bread and continued to boil Lucy's cloth diapers.

Vera gave him grief over everything. The baby could not eat from those disgusting little jars of paste he brought home. She mashed bananas and puréed boiled carrots with a fork. Thank God she'd decided to move with him or the baby would not have made it two weeks without her, she reminded him each day.

He and Ella had been married a little more than a year when Lucy was born in Leningrad, and eight days later the infection that found its way into his wife's bloodstream killed her. His own mother had thought it foolish to abandon the life you knew, and when Yurik left Leningrad, so did she, moving back to the small Ukrainian town where he'd been born. It was Vera who chose to come along, even after Ella had died. She would care for the baby. And it was then Yurik decided he would call her *Mama*.

This morning he had overslept by more than an hour. He wasn't sure how it happened. The alarm must have gone off. Mama must have knocked on his door. All he recalled was the milky stretch of early morning time when he nuzzled closer to his wife.

He tried to crawl in his mind back to where Ella slept, to reach her warmth, but it was impossible so far from his bed, under the twitching lights of that grocery store in his sopping pajamas. And then he thought of his job, wondered whether he would have one tomorrow.

The synagogue would be a mess by now. The services had already started for the day, the Rabbi rocking heel to toe in his pulpit, talking too fast for Yurik to follow. Meanwhile, his wife, dead nearly a year, had tumbled so far beyond his dreams that it would take another day and night of waiting, waking at dawn and forcing himself to sleep again before she would come back, linger in his bed a while, then leave him as always to start his day.

He could never quite see the whole of her those mornings. Ella's face would be so close, yet turned away, and while parts of her pressed against him, others were impossible to grasp. Still, those mornings were the closest he could get to her now that she was gone. In Leningrad, it had been easier. There her smell remained in the sheets; her nightgown lay rumpled under her pillow; her slippers waited at the edge of the bed for her feet.

Rows of baby faces smiled at him, but he did not know which diaper brand to choose. These things—diapers, baby food—were meant to be Ella's matters. Still, he would buy a package of these American diapers. To hell with his mother-in-law. He had a right to wrap his child in whatever he pleased.

He couldn't imagine his life without Lucy now. He'd wake at night and lean over her tiny rising chest in the crib and thank God—the only time he ever did—that she had lived. It had not always been this way. For the first several weeks of Lucy's life, Yurik could not touch her. This wailing thing had grown inside his wife, he'd thought. It flailed its little arms. Gulped air.

On one of those evenings, when Lucy was a month old, Vera left Yurik alone with her for the first time. "Watch the child," she said. She went to the cemetery, as she often did, but this time she did not take Lucy along. Yurik kept to the far corner of the room, away from the wicker crib. Lucy whimpered. She wailed. The sound was unbearable. He gradually edged nearer until he saw her—mouth gaping, eyes crushed into her hot face, chin gathered into a hard red ball. He carried her at arm's length like a pot of boiling water and lay her on the mattress beside him. With the room turned on its side, a certain weight was lifted. He pulled the white gown from under Ella's pillow and draped its folds on Lucy's legs. He could not remember Vera shaking him awake and lifting the sleeping infant from his arms. The next morning he moved the bassinet to his side of the curtain.

Yurik settled on a package of Pampers, but when he reached for his wallet at the counter, he realized he'd left it at home. The cashier's face creased into a wide grin, revealing her few crooked teeth. "Boy or girl?" she asked as she reached across the counter for the diapers.

Yurik jerked his hand away from her. *I have no dollars*, he thought to say, but that would break the spell of his silence.

"He giving you trouble, Ma?" the man called from behind him. Yurik dropped the package on the floor and, as if he'd stolen it, hurried out.

~

It was already past noon. Vera paced the tiny living room, counting. *Five. Four. Three. Two. One. Two. Three. Four. Five. Four. Three. Two. One.* At the end of the round, Yurik would appear, she told herself, but at the end of each round, he did not. He'd been gone nearly five hours and Vera had cycled through every permutation of his whereabouts: Yurik in a gutter, Yurik dragged behind a truck, Yurik floating in the East River.

She peered between the iron bars on the window. The apartment was sweltering, and her cheap polyester skirt plastered itself to the backs of her thighs. The rain had finally cleared and her neighbors filled the benches in their brightly printed housedresses. Vera could join them, but she'd ventured there once not long after moving in and decided never to go back. She'd sat with the women that morning as they talked about food stamps, and FICA, and the price of kvass at the market. Then they lowered their voices. *Did you hear about the one in 4C; her husband dumped her for a Mexican? The drunk from 8G who found his son drowned in the tub?* She left then, abruptly, startling them, imagining their voices turning to her story next—*that woman with the baby. Did you know that's not even her son?*

The metal grating outside the window was splattered in bird droppings. All that bird crap that she could not reach around the glass to clean drove her crazy. Vera hoisted the heavy window up and tried to chip away at the layers of crusted droppings she could get to with a knife. Before they'd left the Soviet Union, she had visited the cemetery in Leningrad nearly every day to clean Ella's plot. Now she could not even put a stone beside her daughter's grave on her birthday. She needed to stay busy all day to keep her mind away from that plot covered in bird shit and mud, Ella alone in the cold earth.

The metal bars were rough and slimy, their rusted black paint flaking off in her hands. Vera would have left the apartment hours ago to take Lucy for a walk, but she worried Yurik would return, realize he'd locked himself out, and vanish again. He knew how to rattle her, running off for hours at a time, never explaining where he went or what he did. At first, she suspected he hid a woman from her, but it seemed unlikely the way he'd go days without washing himself and sulk silently around the apartment. What woman would want any part of that?

Earlier in the morning, she'd resisted pounding on his door, though he was late for work. "I'm a grown man," he'd said to her, indignantly, on more than one occasion when she reminded him of his responsibilities. "Do you think I need another mother?" She'd bitten the inside of her cheek all morning, clamoring around the kitchen, chopping apples as vigorously as she could, banging the pot onto the stove. But a full hour passed before his door opened and he scuffled by in house slippers and pajamas. The front door slammed behind him. His keys hung on their hook, his wallet beneath them. He disappeared down the street in the opposite direction of the synagogue. He'd only started the custodial job with Holy House Cleaners a few weeks before and already he was missing work. Vera had been the one to get him the job. She'd learned the Ukrainian man down the hall ran a cleaning company. *My son*, she'd called Yurik when she cornered the man in the stairwell one evening. It was simpler that way. *My son needs a job,* she'd said, and he'd started the very next week.

An alarm sounded behind her and when she reached her head back into the kitchen, Vera noticed a burning smell. She rushed to the oven, cursing her forgetfulness, finding the cake she'd put in that morning smoldering inside. She flung a rag through the air to silence the alarm and Lucy clapped and giggled at her grandmother's performance.

Birthday or not, what sense was there in baking a cake for a daughter who was dead? Vera scrubbed her hands, filled a bowl with applesauce and set it down in front of Lucy. Normally, she would have fed the child, scraping up the bits of food that squirted from Lucy's lips, but Vera let her have her way with the bowl and spoon. The mess would give her something new to clean.

It was a shame they couldn't go outside. She thought of the streets in Rome, where they'd waited six months for their paperwork to continue to New York, when she'd filled her days with walking. That stretch of time after a rainfall when the cobbled roads were still damp had been her favorite—everything slick and newly cleaned.

Not long after they arrived, she'd befriended a young woman named Olga and together they circled the Piazza Navona, pushing their strollers. Olga had identical twin boys and Vera was drawn to her because of them.

She never told Olga that Lucy had also been a twin, her brother, a bundle of blue limbs delivered dead, moments before her. Some things you kept private.

Vera remembered one of their last walks now, how she and Olga held tightly to their strollers that afternoon, the cobbled street slippery from a heavy shower.

"Did you get along with your son's wife?" Olga had asked on that walk. "My husband's mother never liked me, not even after the babies were born."

"She was my daughter," Vera corrected her.

"You must have been close," Olga said. "Renata would never call me her daughter."

Vera understood then what others had assumed. Why else would Yurik leave Leningrad with her if he weren't her son?

"Yes. Very close," she said.

"Before we moved, my mother-in-law was always complaining I raised the twins all wrong," Olga said.

Vera felt the same regret now in her claustrophobic kitchen as she'd felt walking with Olga—the wish that she had defended Ella each time Yurik's mother criticized her. *Your daughter wears too much makeup; she talks to too many men; she can't cook.*

"Ella and I were very close," Vera said.

"How did she die?" Olga asked.

"An infection in her blood. I couldn't leave Yurik to raise Lucy alone."

"Of course. What mother would do such a thing?"

That was when Vera had decided it would be easiest to continue this way.

"No," she said. "I could never leave my son."

A bus hissed to a stop on Ocean Parkway, releasing a long metallic groan. Lucy squealed in her booster chair. *Babu babu babu,* she cried. Applesauce dribbled from her chin, coating her little fists and streaking her hair. Vera smiled at Lucy's obliviousness to the mess. She was so much like her mother had been at this age; same flushed full cheeks, same tuft of bronze curls, eyes that seemed to take in all the light. Vera sat Lucy at the edge of the sink and bathed her hands and face as she'd done with Ella all those years ago. She was fifty-one, and a new mother all over again.

Big girl you are, she said in Russian as she dried Lucy off and hoisted her on her hip. *Big.* Bounce. *Big.* Bounce. *Big.* She pressed her nose into the apple smell that lingered on Lucy's soft infant flesh. When she was born, Vera had held her like a tiny bird in her cupped hands. Now she was a sturdy baby, dimpled at her elbows and wrists.

Chubby like your Mama was. Lucy sniffled, froze, and knit her faint brows like a grown woman. *Ma. Ma. Ma,* she sang and reached for the floor to be let down. She gurgled and chattered in her made-up tongue. Some moments it seemed to Vera that Lucy could sense her brother nearby. She would talk as though to someone beside her, lay her toys on the ground as if to share, stare out as though listening to a voice only she could hear. It was absurd, Vera knew. This was the way children played, but she couldn't stop herself from imagining the little boy there some days, what it would have been like to have two.

Vera paced the room, checked her watch. 12:43. *How do they bury the dead here? Boxed up in cardboard like a carton of eggs? Do they eat McDonald's afterward? It must be expensive—the casket, the Rabbi, the guests.*

Vera scrubbed the table and counters once more. She dried the inside of the sink. Yurik drove her crazy but that aggravation filled the space her memory would otherwise invade. They did that for each other —distracted grief with anger, frustration.

There was nothing left to keep her hands busy. Vera lifted Lucy, strapped her into her stroller. Ella was alone in the earth all those thousands of miles away. But Yurik, where was he? The not-knowing was too much. She had to get away from that apartment. She had to get out.

~

His feet were aching now. He must have been walking for hours, though he hadn't made it far from home. Time didn't move the way it ought to anymore. Just the other day, Ella showed up at his army base in Siberia. She'd worn a lavender silk dress, the green of her eyes brighter than he had ever seen before. The other men in his unit whistled and yelped when she arrived. "Hands off," he'd proudly announced. "That's my wife."

The sky had cleared but his house slippers were still soaked. The boulevard was busy again. At the corner, a busty woman with her hair wrapped in a violet-printed scarf knelt over a fire hydrant. When her body heaved, a spray of water shot across the street, a cluster of pigeons sprang up from the sidewalk, and Yurik froze at the curb, the water misting his arms with tiny crystals. Two small children in matching underpants shrieked and leaped across the foaming blast, and the woman reclined against a stoop, fanning herself with a newspaper. Her relief was a kind familiar to him since he'd become a father—those moments, Lucy fiddling with a spoon or sock, when he could untether his attention from her. But the children reminded him of another time, of dancing with Ella across the wet stones under the mushroom fountain in Petergof. He smiled at that memory of Ella—her damp curls pressed like vines to her back, her lithe figure spinning under a canopy of water.

Two figures stood in front of him, huddling close to one another. The children had stopped their hopping and studied him. Yurik realized what a sight he must be—his T-shirt had a hole the size of an apple just below the neckline and his pants clung to his legs. The woman on the stoop called the children over, placed a hand on each of their shoulders, and stared at Yurik.

He rushed away. It was no use trying to find any calm here. He would go to the park. On the way, he passed a bum who slept on a bench, a dirty arm dangling to the ground. A young couple threw hunks of bread in the pond. Geese pecked at the fat white crumbs, and others scrambled toward them from the water, still others calling shrilly from the sky. A woman in a white uniform paced at the edge of the pond, spitting into the water, her hands on her hips. A group of teenaged black boys bounced a ball, darting on their feet. Their swift movements dizzied him.

Yurik picked a spot beneath a tree, curled on his side against the mossy roots that poked up from the dirt, and shut his eyes. He was eager to sleep, but that woman by the pond had reminded him of his mother. It wasn't just the uniform that resembled his mother's nursing clothes. It was the spitting—precisely the kind of inelegance that made her harshness more crass than Mama's. His mother had always been suspicious of the girls Yurik went with and was never shy about voicing her disapproval, a flaw that only deepened when he married.

When he went to Siberia for his army service not long after the wedding, his mother wrote him often. *Your wife does not always wear her wedding ring. I caught her smoking a cigarette with a man outside the apteka. She puts on red lipstick now. She bought lace underpants. Where does the money come from?*

He wrote to Ella. *What's all this my mother says?* A month later she arrived at his base, wearing that silk dress. Weeks later, when she wrote to tell him she was pregnant, he'd been thrilled.

But even that his mother had managed to spoil. *Your wife is getting too big*, she wrote. *When did she visit? May? She looks much farther along. What if it's not your child? A son can trust only his mother for the truth.*

Something was burning. Yurik opened his eyes. A bare-chested man stirred the coals in a nearby grill and the smoke wafted toward him. Yurik coughed and rolled onto his back. A mass of white clouds receded quickly, the sun breaking into view so that a maze of bright spots darted across his vision. He shut his eyes and the sun pressed like a purple bruise beneath his lids. Ella *had* visited just that one time in May. Once you got a thought planted in your head, you couldn't drive it out. Only in the hospital months later, did he find out Ella had been so large because she had been carrying twins and then there was, of course, the guilt of having ever questioned her, the anger at his mother—all of it come too late.

It was impossible to be in love and see a person whole. His wife lived in that lavender dress now. She lived in the summer palace, on sidewalks in Leningrad, her hand hidden inside his coat pocket, or breathing close beside him in bed when it was dark enough only to feel, not see her there.

The ground thudded against the back of his head—the ball bouncing against the pavement between the boys' darting feet. The woman by the pond was gone. The geese had dispersed; the couple sat at the edge of the water; the bum on the bench shifted onto his side. Yurik closed his eyes again. The rhythmic thumping was almost soothing. It lulled him to sleep.

Ella lay there beside him, so much softness that he did not know where to put his hands. She shivered and he pulled her close. Her heart beat loudly through her back against his chest, as though an echo of his own heart outside of himself.

"The wind. There's so much wind," she whispered. He tried to keep her from shaking, laced his fingers between hers.

"I feel him," she said. She was feverish. "I feel our son still inside me. He's kicking. He just hasn't come out yet."

Her spine pressed close into him. "He's right here, Yurik." She glided his hand, against the soft loose flesh of her belly where the muscles were all gone, the skin so stretched from pregnancy that it felt nothing like the taut young body he'd once known.

Yurik's desire for her in that moment ached inside of him. He longed for this soft animal of his wife who writhed and panted against him. "Feel that? It's his heartbeat," she insisted. "He's right here."

Yurik ran his hand along that loose flesh and wanted to fold himself inside of her. Then he noticed something tiny and hot wriggling beside Ella's breasts. A little damp fist gripped his thumb. Lucy. He placed a hand gently on the baby's head, against the soft spot where the halves of her skull did not yet meet. A small gasp rose from Ella. Yurik barely breathed, afraid to break the membrane of that moment, frail as a spider's web wavering against the wind.

And then there was a sudden stabbing at his stomach, a kick so swift it choked the air from his lungs. Ella's face was over him—the gray-green eyes, the curve of her lip—but as he blinked away his sleep, the face became an ugly thing, working itself into contortions. It shouted—not words but sounds, like some massive creature tugging hard and mad off the end of a chain collar—wanting to choke and run free all at once.

His breath returned to him. The trees and grass and sky around him came into focus, but he was not yet certain if he was awake. At his feet, sat his child. She kicked her legs like they might lift her out of her stroller, flapping her arms, scrunching her nose, her voice high and thin like a seagull's call, accompanying her grandmother's shouting.

Vera moved with something deep inside herself she could not still, a tiny buried throbbing thing. She had not thought as she'd plowed Lucy's stroller through the soft wet earth, had not thought as her foot caught against his gut, as the words not even she could make out poured from her. The feeling rose and knocked at the cage of her ribs, but when she tried to kick it back, it knotted in her throat. She'd first noticed it in the windowless hospital room where they'd spent Ella's last hours—a stretch of time unpunctured by the movement of the sun. Every night since then, she would lay awake and think what she'd thought when she had let Ella's hands loose that day: *tomorrow he'll be gone*. Every morning after Ella's death when they had lived in Leningrad, she would rise, pull the curtain between them back, expecting Yurik's bed to be abandoned. Each time she found him curled on his side, she fought the impulse to kneel beside him, take his hand. She loathed that need, would holler at him to drown it out.

Yurik did not scramble away from her or even recoil from her kick, but stared up, bewildered by the anger. Lucy stretched her plump hands out, shrieking. He lifted her from her seat and pressed her softness to him. She quieted in his arms, her breath quick and irregular.

The sight of his clumsy hands, so careful now with the child, silenced Vera. She thought of the moment that last day when she'd reached across her daughter's corpse, allowing him to take hold of her hand. She shut her eyes and the feeling thrummed between her temples now—a need greater than the sum of her stubbornness and anger. She felt her knees like snapping twigs, the damp earth receiving her, the sturdiness of his frame at her side, and held still.

Yurik examined the angular bones; the raised purple veins forking across Vera's hands and rested his palm atop them. He was awake now and awake in him was the relief that she had brought his child, that he did not have to lay alone in the cold wet earth.

A skein of geese passed overhead, squawking at one another to stay close. Lucy's breath fluttered and caught at her throat, her arms and legs twitching against his chest. He touched his lips to her silky hair. "Sleep, sleep," he said softly into the top of her head. "I'm right here."

New Year's Eve

Dan Langton

We know who's dying, not who's being born;
a boy who kills his mother as he's torn
from her will redeem the world, a dancer
we can tell from the dance, while the answer
we have dearly sought will come from a girl
in Uzbekistan. A flag will unfurl.
Our Mozart will give us a threnody,
a hint of Lincoln, or of Kennedy.

Tonight so many look into the past,
the dusk, the useless rooms, the die they cast,
to see the time when they will be alone,
when they will put the stone upon the stone;
they should be buoyant, even as they mourn,
we know who's dying, not who's being born.

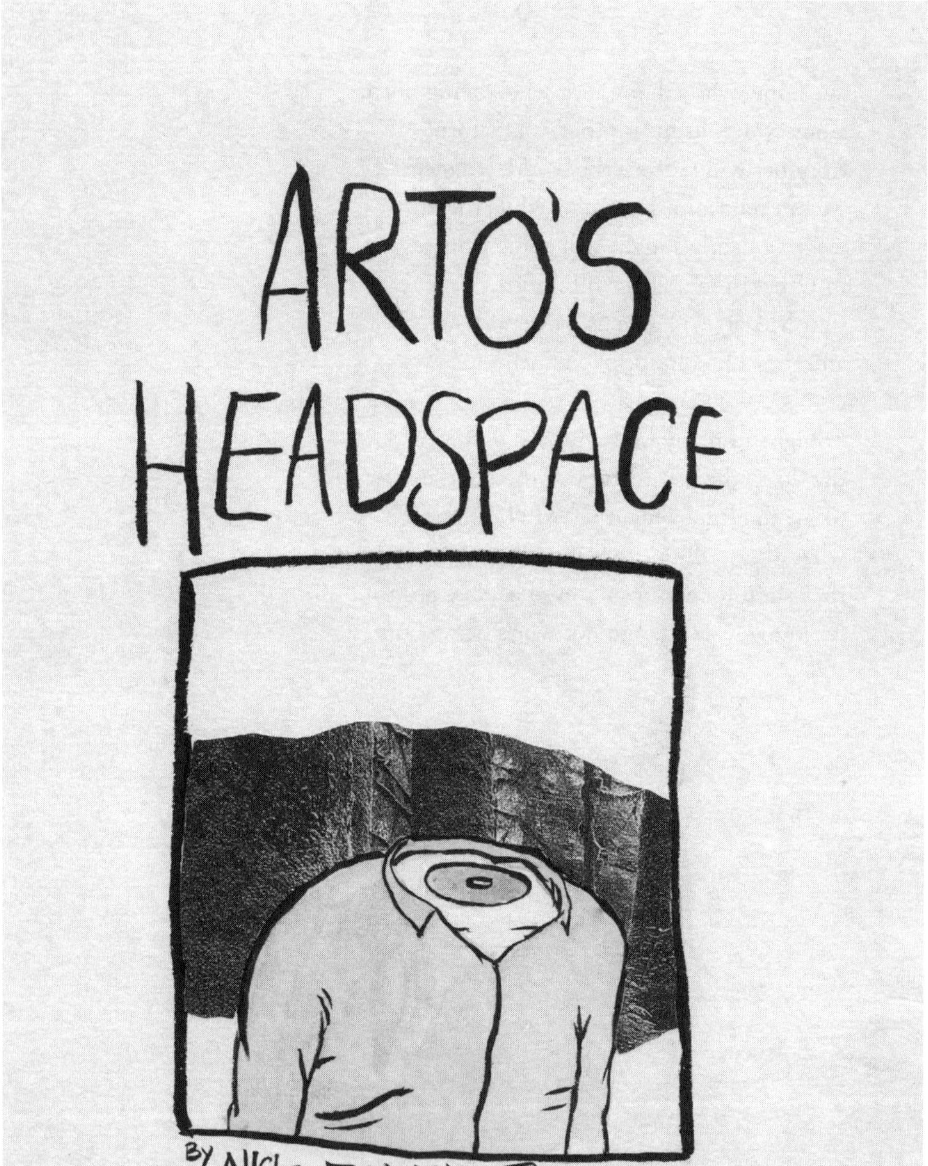
ARTO'S HEADSPACE
BY NICK FRANCIS POTTER

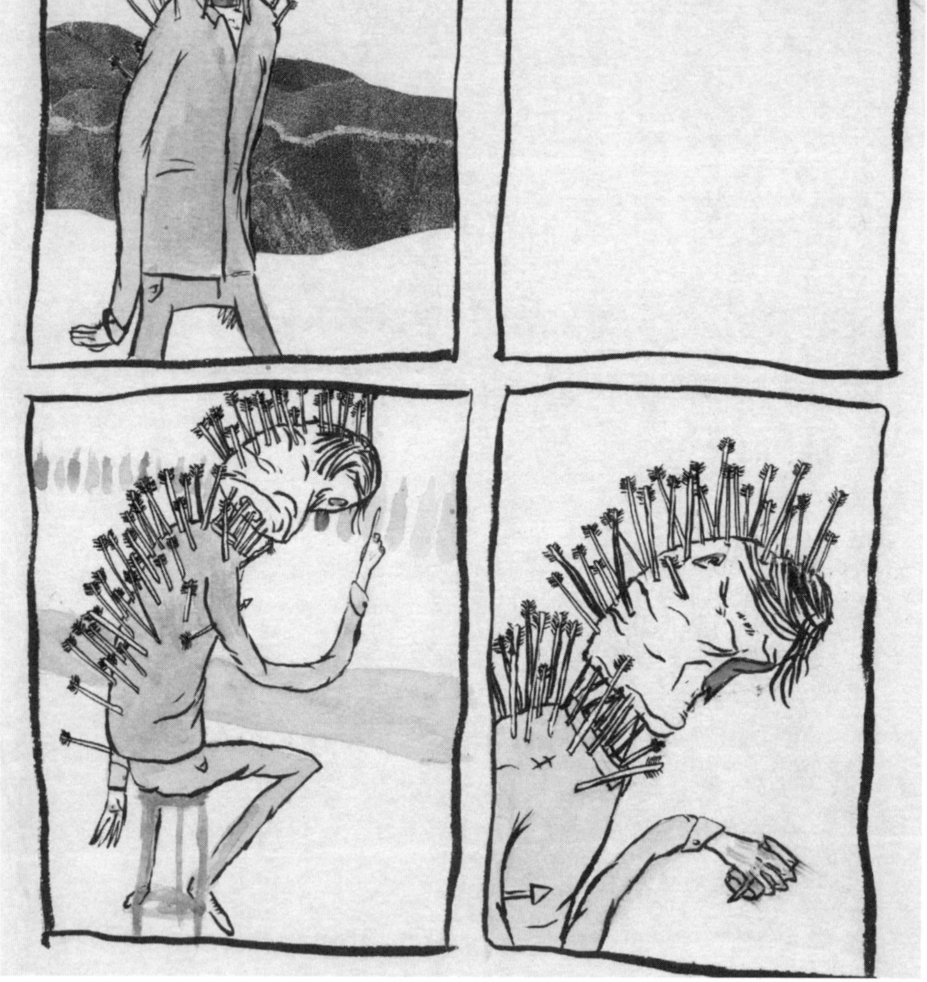

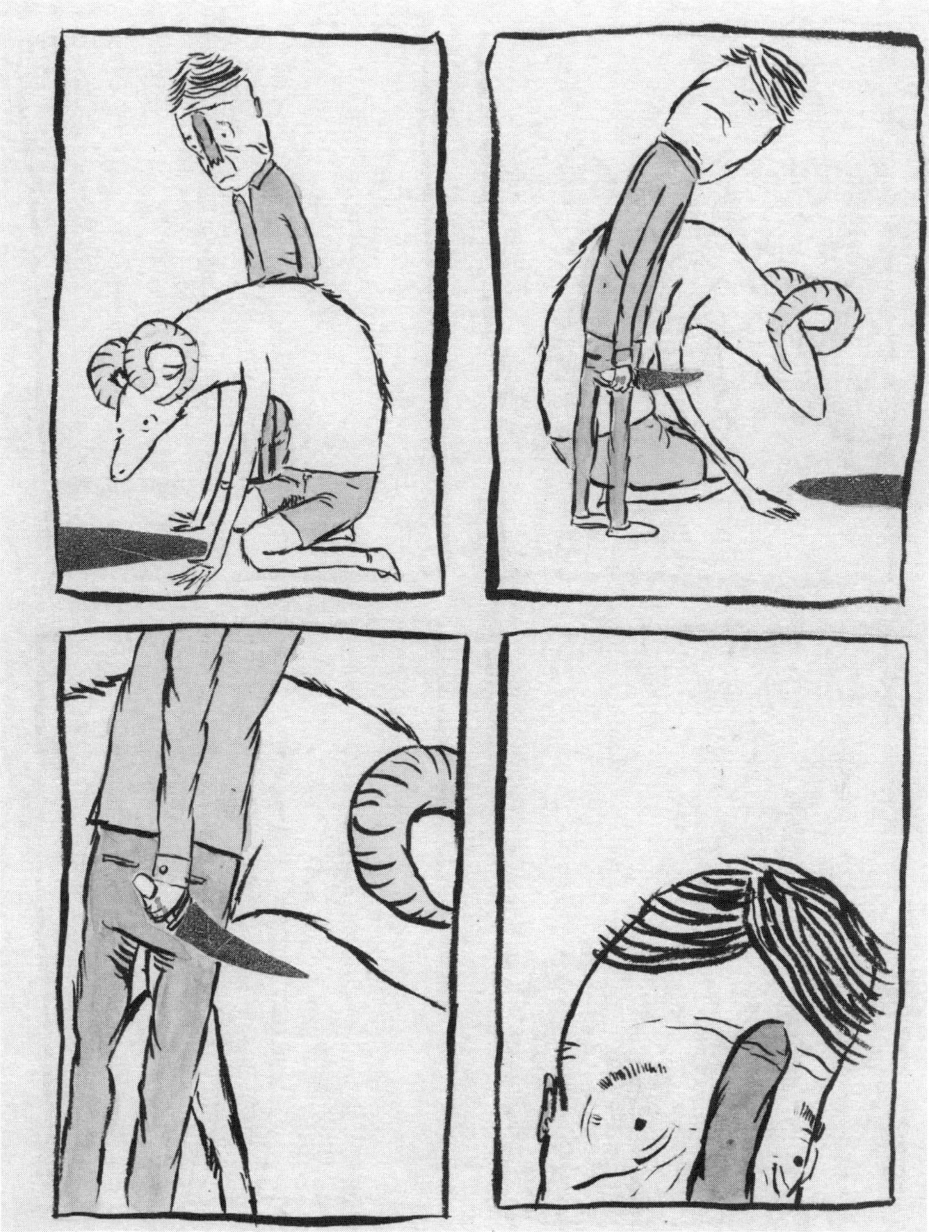

fin.

Ode to Iowa City

Agatha Beins

When neon is your guide and *24 hours* blinks
pink

blank

pink. When limbs sigh punctuated
by mulberries that soften and drop just
slightly toward the river's current,
its uneven pull only suggested by a contradiction
of shadows. When glass breaks unwitnesssed.
In the earliest sliver of morning two eggs
sunny-side-up are a bright simulacrum: the white
too clean, the orange too eager.
Dreams are flayed, open

letting us bear witness to the breath, to the space
made before pupils turn to explain
the dark. Let apricot lights hum
tinny and humid. Let imperfection comfort
the perception of distance and its lack,
where *near* curls tongue-tied into *flush* and

you might again choose, this time
to not look back. Hymns for the present, the underlying
cause, the echo. Let each find its own
fiction. Let staples clutch
the weathered telephone pole like shiny arachnid
legs left mid-climb and bodiless. Against the first birds
of morning we always age gracefully and the bruises we offer
each other as gifts appear always tomorrow.

Memphis Soul Hour

John Warner Smith

Nights my grandpa gambled,
grandma laid awake
with her rosary beads
draped to the bed post.
Dragging heavy, crusted
feet, she'd rise to open
her door, squeaking,
and let all the bone heat
of hell fly. Chewing clumps
of corn starch, she'd rattle
her teeth like a tin can.
On the living room couch
two daughters slump
with their lovers
while Memphis Soul crackles
softly in the blue-lit dark.
Sultry and sweaty, they slither
like snakes between
whispers and a sex wish.
Then, a tongue spewing
holy water and fire,
a soliloquy of cuss and prayer
seething like boiling grits.
Sheetrock walls shimmy,
porch screen hinges pop,
and a breeze cools the house.

Nursemaids

~

Michelle Valois

Named after the queen
who raised her voice and saved
a people, Esther translates
gestures of grief and wordless
pleas for more blankets, less
noise. Noah builds his ship and sails
away. I watch him wave at passing
doves and receive his souvenir
tissue boxes stacked four high
by my bed, delivered when he thinks
I am asleep and when I pretend to be.
Ari, the lion-hearted, whose roar
can wake the dead and often does,
studies the tube that feeds
his mother and never looks away.

Cross Sound Ferry

David O'Connell

It was raining, we played
cribbage, wet dogs
snuffled past. It was more
than an hour to Orient Point.
We'd be married
in a month. It wasn't romantic
to live with her parents.
Not sexy to sleep under
Wham! posters. That summer
the country parsed worry
with color. She proofed
resumes. I couldn't sleep.
The heave wasn't much,
but it got to me. Our car
in the hull was off limits.
The PSAs urged us to
say something. Bubbles
or rice for the church steps?
Armstrong or James
for the dance? She shuffled,
dealt. A couple at the rail
braved one umbrella
for their cigarette.

Dissolution

~

Jared Pearce

I've tracked this clam-shell
Snowflake down
To the tongues of the just
Greened lawn where I guess
The leaves must feel as I did
When I first had a rice candy
And the wrapper dissolved
In my mouth, or the shock
Of tossing a styrofoam
Cup into the campfire:
The known world stripped
To its strands, then gone,
And me wondering if
It were ever there at all?

Pennsylvania Dutch

Noel Sloboda

Every April the stories changed,
but the ritual remained the same

as I sealed beds behind Nana's place,
covering rain-soaked ground

under layers of black and white print—
a foundation for loads of mulch.

Nana saved her papers for months,
stacked headlines about ice storms,

holiday sales and pep rallies
atop classifieds and obituaries.

As I laid out pages capturing
everything that mattered

during the shortest days of the year,
I made sure all aligned to ring

the house with a winter hex
warding off spring weeds.

Yet my rough magic never prevented
eruptions of ivy and oxalis

I spent June ripping out.
As Nana watched me work,

she muttered German curses—
more mox nix words

brought from another world
powerless over profane ground.

A Place Called Sickness

Sean Carswell

The old woman and her daughter were sitting on their porch when Mr. Langkjaer drove up their road for the last time. The old woman, Regina Cline O'Connor, leaned heavy on the right arm of her white rocking chair and craned her neck for a better look at Mr. Langkjaer's shiny Ford ambling down the leaf-strewn driveway. A peacock blocked Mr. Langkjaer's path. Mr. Langkjaer's Ford slowed to a pace that questioned the very notion of the word motion. It seemed as if forward could shift into reverse without any demonstrative change in progress. The peacock would not hurry. The Ford could not inspire a greater pace in the fowl. The peacock knew his privilege on the farm. Other drivers had confronted the birds, coming close enough to run their tires over the long tail feathers. This was a crime that Mr. Langkjaer knew he could not commit. The old woman's daughter, Flannery, prized these peacocks more than the chicken she had trained to walk backwards two decades earlier. Flannery claimed the eye at the peak of the peacock's tail feathers was the eye of the Almighty come forth to deliver divine grace. Regina doubted it. Regina felt that her daughter simply liked the odd birds, Flannery being an odd bird herself.

Flannery the odd bird did not look up to watch the approaching Ford. She continued to plunk away on her ukulele. Regina found the music to be grotesque. It had its roots in old-time gospel and the Appalachian picking of Regina's childhood, but something else had crept in, something Regina had heard vibrating around the Negro cabins on the back forty acres. The kids of Flannery's generation called this music bluegrass. Regina knew better. She knew jazz when she heard it. Flannery's tiny fingers bounced about the strings and fret board. Regina shook her head. Where was the melody? Where was the word of the Lord in this racket?

Mr. Langkjaer parked the Ford adjacent to the front porch. He stepped out of the car and brushed the wrinkles off his gray flannel suit. The old woman watched every move. Mr. Langkjaer raised his fedora and nodded. Regina nodded back. Mr. Langkjaer started up the brick path to the porch. The profile of his face was a crescent moon on the wane. What her daughter saw in this Danish textbook salesman was beyond anything Regina could quite possibly comprehend. The man called his sample book with the tables of contents for the textbooks he sold his "bible." Mr. Langkjaer never called the real Bible at all. He strolled with no greater pace than the peacock had shown earlier. Neither man nor bird, thought Regina, knows a mortal sin from a can of Shinola. Both of them wear their pride like a birthright. "I best see about dinner," Regina said. She stood from the rocker and walked inside.

Flannery played her bluegrass ukulele to the beat of Mr. Langkjaer's footsteps, slowing the rhythm as he walked the brick steps leading up to the porch. He opened the screen door without a word. Flannery set the ukulele down and said, simply, "Erik." She gathered her courage. Her day's first challenge would be her rise from this chair. The lupus in her blood threatened to kill her, and the adrenocorticotropic hormone she'd been taking for the past three years leached the marrow from her hip bones. When she stood or when she lay flat, she felt that her life could contain perhaps as much future as it had past, that tomorrows could outnumber yesterdays. When she bent to sit, or bent to stand, she felt that she'd aged three years for every one she lived. The process of standing took her from a twenty-nine-year old girl to an eighty-seven-year-old woman. She bent to stand for Erik. The pain coursed through her. She wobbled for a second on her feet. Erik engulfed her in a hug that was perhaps more supportive than romantic.

Elements of the Old South continued to live at the O'Connor farm. Regina's brother had dubbed the land "Andalusia." White tenant farmers continued to work the front twenty acres. African Americans—"Negroes," as Regina called them in her more diplomatic moments—worked the back forty. The house itself, while far from the plantation mansions of old, retained the thick white columns and broad front porch of a bygone era. An ancient magnolia from a time when Milledgeville was the capitol of antebellum Georgia shaded the house. Every noon, Mrs. Freeman, the white wife of the tenant farmer on the front twenty acres, cooked a formal dinner. If only Regina and her daughter were present, then the two ate with four empty dining room chairs. If company were present, leaves could be inserted into the table and up to six guests could join. Mrs. Freeman dined by herself in the kitchen, and only after the O'Connors and their guests were finished.

The ghost of a ham haunted today's dinner. The black-eyed peas had been slow cooked with the ham bone. Ham fat flavored the collard greens. Even the lard in the cornbread contained hints of salted pork. The main dish, of course, was the best and heaviest part of the ham: its butt end. Mrs. Freeman doled carefully measured spoonfuls of the beans and greens onto the plates of both Regina and Erik. The portions, like the plates that contained them, were small. Flannery's doctor had placed her on a no-salt diet, so she could not join Erik and Regina in the ham-haunted dinner. Mrs. Freeman served her a bland vegetable soup. Flannery scooped the wilted collards out of the thin broth with a wry smile.

Regina said, "Mr. Langkjaer, I expect you plan to take my daughter for another of your famous rides?"

Erik chewed the dry cornbread until it formed a paste in his mouth, then washed it down with sweetened iced tea so full of sugar that it was more syrup than beverage. He cleared his throat. "Well, then, there, Mrs. O'Connor." Erik kept his white cloth napkin close to his mouth to keep the corn bread crumbs from spreading. "I don't know how famous these rides are or what they're famous for, but your daughter has shown me a great deal of the world around Milledgeville, and I look forward to her further tutelage."

"And I expect you don't have a chaperone to take with you," Regina said.

"No," Erik said. "No chaperone."

Regina corrected Erik in her mind: *No, ma'am. I have no chaperone.* Erik scooped a forkful of black-eyed peas into his mouth in what he thought was a friendly manner. He had no way of knowing the offense he caused with his lack of a "ma'am." Erik Langkjaer had learned to speak English in a Danish elementary school. The English was an English dialect. Colloquialisms of the American South were unheard.

Never had the word ma'am been uttered that far north of Copenhagen.

Flannery, for her part, had fought this battle with her mother many times. Neither side ever declared victory. There was no point in fighting one more time, and in front of Erik. She ate her salt-free soup and said all she could through her silence.

Regina knew about this Mr. Langkjaer, though. Flannery did not know men. Regina did. She'd married Flannery's father. And it taught Regina an important lesson. Men leave. All men leave. It's in the nature of a man to leave. Her husband Edward had left without having to go anywhere to do it. He didn't even bother to get out of bed to die. He just lay right there in their marriage bed, soul gone to heaven and corpse chilling Regina when she awoke. He could blame the lupus, sure. Flannery would blame that same silent killer. But he left, sure as the day is long. And so would this Mr. Langkjaer. As sure as the pointy nose on his crescent moon of a face, he'd leave. She didn't know for certain that this was the last time he'd visit. She sensed it would be, though.

After dinner, the old woman chaperoned Erik and Flannery as far as the front porch. Flannery carried her ukulele in her right hand and held Erik's elbow with her left hand. The longer she continued the adrenocorticotropic hormone treatments, the more her joints seemed to creak, the more her bones seemed to disintegrate. If Erik had much walking in mind, Flannery would have to subtly suggest a walking stick. Twenty-nine years old may be far to young for a girl to need a cane, but Flannery knew that the hip needs what the hip needs. She leaned on Erik's elbow as lightly as she could while walking down the steps. If Erik noticed, he said nothing about Flannery's heavy hand. He pointed to a strand of flowers surrounding a nearby live oak. "Your geraniums are lovely."

Flannery smiled. Bless Erik's heart. He couldn't tell the difference between a bush and a tree, much less between geraniums and chrysanthemums. He did know Flannery's stories, though, which was more than Regina could say. For Regina, the fact that Flannery wrote short stories was something short of a scandal, but more than an embarrassment. She would never understand what kind of lady would think so much of herself to think that her daydreams needed to be written down and typed up and sent out into the world. It was nothing short of indecent.

Erik trafficked in fiction, though. He travelled from university to university, selling these daydreams in textbooks and anthologies. He knew the daydreams Flannery would share, and he knew the first one. It had been a little story named "The Geraniums." And so, on Flannery's front yard, any flower must be a geranium. Even if it was this deep into fall and geraniums never survived that first October cold snap. Even if autumn blooms with that deep yellow had to be a chrysanthemum. Flannery said, "It's not so literal."

Erik helped her down the final step and onto the brick walkway. A peacock bellowed. Erik winced. No matter how many times he'd heard these fowl cry, they always sounded like a wounded child to him. "What's not so literal?" he asked.

"The geraniums," Flannery said. "You can know me a little from my fiction, but I don't tell the whole story."

Erik nodded. They moseyed down the brick path to Erik's Ford. Erik opened the passenger door for Flannery. She and her ukulele settled into the front seat. Erik shut the door behind them and sauntered over to his own door. Time seemed to run at a slower pace on these Milledgeville autumn afternoons.

Flannery guided Erik down the various dirt roads, through farms and fields, pecan plantations and second-growth southern pines that locals looked at as lumber more than trees. For someone who never drove and seemed to lose more mobility every time Erik came to visit, Flannery knew every back road of this county. She could navigate him directly into the Gothic past and the hidden beauty. Forget country. This place was a whole different planet from the Denmark Erik knew as a boy. He gawked and asked questions, amazed to find that Flannery could name every tree and distinguish the tupelos from the poplars, the loblolly pines from slash pines, the sweetgums from the black walnuts. Flannery could tell the story of the old white man trudging along the road, lugging a wood box of carpentry tools and Erik could even believe that Flannery knew the old man and that the story was real.

For her part, Flannery kept thumbing through the book of samples that Erik called his bible. She noticed Emily Dickinson's poetry was finding a home in more and more anthologies these days. Just ten years ago, when Flannery attended the Georgia State College for Women, Dickinson was little more than a footnote in literature classes. Flannery had learned about Dickinson from a history professor, of all people. Helen Greene. The very same woman who had introduced Erik and Flannery. "You selling more Emily Dickinson these days?" Flannery asked.

"You know we don't sell individual authors," Erik said. He stole a glance at Flannery. Her gaze was still locked on the bible. In moments like these, when her smile didn't push up the cheeks that were swollen by hormone treatments, with her glasses off and no sense of eyes upon her, Flannery was something like a beautiful young woman. Erik may not have been in love, but he was aware that Flannery was a woman and he wanted to kiss her. Instead, he turned his eyes back to the dirt road in time to swerve around a startled squirrel. He added, "You're a little bit like that Emily Dickinson."

Flannery clenched her jaw. "How so?"

"Living out your days in your family home, watching over your mother in her old age…"

"My mother is not that old."

"…writing these enigmatic little pieces about God and redemption. You could be the twentieth century's own little virgin poet."

Flannery whipped not only her gaze but her whole body so that she sat facing him across the bench seat. Erik had never seen such speed, such agility out of her. He wondered if he'd said the wrong thing, if she might pounce upon him. She glared at Erik, perhaps wondering the same thing. Instead, she produced her ukulele and began to strum a few simple chords. "Greensleeves," she said. She played through the melody. It sounded somewhat soft, but she played with enough force and confidence to be heard over the wind flowing in through the windows. She strummed as she said, "Every Emily Dickinson poem can be sung to the tune of 'Greensleeves.'"

And, to prove her point, Flannery sang first about a narrow fellow in the grass and second about a visit from death, all while playing the same simple melody. When she started into "Wild nights, wild nights!" in that notoriously thick Southern accent of hers, Erik slowed the car to a crawl and parked under a stand of hickories. He listened to Flannery sing about the wild nights that could be their luxury. When she stopped, he said, "With your permission, I would like to kiss you."

Flannery, of course, was no Emily Dickinson. She would not hide behind a curtain and listen to music in another room. She would not lock herself in her room when a suitor came calling. She may not be the most experienced romantic in Baldwin County, and she may be a devout Catholic, but she would not be defined as the twentieth century's own little virgin poet. She spoke softly. "You have my permission."

Erik closed his eyes and leaned in. Later, he would read Flannery's fictionalized version of this kiss. She described the adrenaline that surged through her, the same type that enables a girl to carry a packed trunk out of a burning house. But for Erik, all he felt was awkward. Flannery didn't know how to position her lips, so he ended up kissing her teeth. He grazed his hand softly across her ribs. He could feel the crumbling bones underneath her wool coat, each rib jutting like the ridges in the dirt roads they'd ridden along. The teeth. The ribs. Flannery's sickness flooded through Erik. Where he wanted to feel love, he felt death.

He was at a loss. Should he keep kissing her teeth? Could he stop? Erik dangled over the precipice of panic for one second, then another until, luckily, the sound of a man clearing his throat drifted through the open window. Erik released Flannery. They both turned to see the man who had wandered up behind the parked car. He was a lean white man in his late fifties. He pushed back a black felt hat ringed with sweat. "Y'all doing okay?" he asked. "Ain't got a flat tire or nothing, do you?"

"No, sir," Erik said. "Everything is just fine."

"Well, okay, then." The old man nodded and started again on his way down the road.

Flannery, for her part, could not stop giggling. Clearly, she was just plain tickled by the whole affair.

Unfortunately, Flannery was so flustered when Erik dropped her back off at Andalusia that she forgot her ukulele in his car. The next she heard from him, he'd taken a six-month leave of absence from work and returned to Denmark. Whether or not he took her ukulele with him is not clear. Either way, both were gone.

The autumn turned to winter and the subsequent spring limped in without the usual sense of rebirth. Flannery's doctor took her off the adrenocorticotropic hormone and put her on an experimental drug called Meticorton. Flannery's thirtieth birthday came with a cane that she would need to get around that summer. One year after the kiss, Flannery purchased the pair of aluminum crutches that she'd ride for the rest of her life. These crutches helped her out to the mailbox, where she found her final letter from Erik: the one in which he announced his engagement.

Flannery stuffed the letter in the pocket of her wool coat and hobbled through the magnolias and live oaks, the chrysanthemums back in bloom and the sweetgums carpeting pathways with their falling leaves until she made it well into the back forty of Andalusia, to a shack that an old black man had built, that Regina knew nothing about and everyone else ignored. The man's name was Coleman. Flannery liked him because he had skin that wrapped around a bag of bones in the same ill-fated manner as Flannery's. She, too, turned a blind eye to the moonshine still he used to make his money. She tapped on his door with the rubber end of her crutch. Coleman groaned and cursed his popping knee joints and kicked over a tin plate that never should have been left on the floor to begin with and eventually opened the door. Of course, he would've known from the knock that it was Flannery and of course he would've known what she was there for. He invited her in. He lit the fire in his little chimney and set a kettle on to boil. He asked, "Would you like some coffee, Miss Flannery?"

"Yes, please, Coleman." She lowered herself into an old cane chair next to Coleman's one table. She hesitated to ask. Surely, Coleman would get to the matter in his own time. She leaned the crutches against the back of her chair and folded her hands in her lap. She could still feel the crumpled letter in her coat.

Coleman watched the kettle come to a boil, then set two mugs of coffee on a slow drip. He smiled wide enough for Flannery to catch a glimpse of his foremost tooth: the lower right canine. He reached from behind a chest of drawers and pulled out his latest work of art: a cigar box ukulele made for his favorite dying girl. He handed it over.

Flannery grazed her fingers across the frets, tapped the soundboard of old, dry redwood, and tuned the strings. It wasn't quite the masterpiece of dark mahogany and tortoiseshell binding that she'd left in Erik's car, but it was beautiful in all the ways it seemed so fallen and lacking. Flannery worried that, if she looked up to smile at Coleman, she'd cry. Coleman said, "Play us a song for our suffering, Flannery."

Flannery plucked through the scale of C, eight simple notes, then let her fingers leap and dance across the fret board. It was a song from a place of sickness. A place where there is no company. Where nobody can follow.

It Hurts My Teeth

Meredith Luby

I'm worried about the kittens in my wall. I hear their soft mewing at night. Their tiny claws leave dents in the plaster. It is possible that they're pigeons, or maybe wrens. The noises are muffled, the scratching ambiguous. What I think is the pounding of paws against the wall could be the beating of wings, trying and failing to go anywhere. If anyone bothered to lay their head against my wall they'd hear it too. Maybe. I'm patient. I can wait for the day the wall cracks and they find their way free and everyone is proven wrong. This is an old house. It won't be much longer now.

My boyfriend and I sat in a coffee shop and I pulled off my thumbnails. I walked behind him and stroked the back of his ear. His denim shirt was old, deteriorating. It slumped on the blades of his shoulders like the rind of a half peeled orange. By the time my nails grow back I'm sure the cats will have found their way out. My left thumbnail still hung on like a dying orchid blossom. Later, while I took off my shirt, it freed itself. Clinging to white cotton, I wouldn't find it until a few days later when I did laundry.

It's not like there was a lot of blood. They were bruised and calloused and came off without too much pain or trouble. Jack slammed the door on my hands last week when I stopped suddenly because I heard the cats. Not on purpose. If they're birds I don't think they'll live much longer. But kittens could stick it out. Everyone has seen those mangy ones on the street and at least inside my wall they're safe from the rain.

I tried reading Jack's palms. His fingers are knobbed, like a much older man. It didn't work because I couldn't remember which line was which, and also my nail-less thumbs weird him out. If he had let me finish I would've told him what palm readers always say. That the life line is long and the love line crosses a lot. I would've thrown in that he'd have three children because I know he wants none. I don't believe in that stuff but I'd like other people to believe. I don't think I love him but I've made a game of seeing how long I can pretend I do. Some day soon I'll get so caught up in the pretending that the love will be real. That's how it should work, anyway.

My mother lives far away but I hardly ever miss her. Sometimes I miss my bedroom in her house with its big windows. And sometimes I miss watching her cook dinner, her long hair in a braid twisted into a knot at the nape of her neck. It seems like a long time ago that I left but it may have only been last week. She had a drawl that embarrassed me during parent teacher conferences. Sometimes Jack will do an imitation of it. We still live in the south but not in a place where people talk like her. I laugh but I don't like thinking of her as a caricature, the way he does. I think of her sharp elbows and floral dresses. She made me ones just like them. She would be sad that I dyed my hair. That I wear stockings with holes in them by choice.

I thought living in a house like this one would be very different from the orderly one I came from. But really it's just that old paint chips stick to my feet. And the kittens. There wouldn't have been a way for them to get in at my mother's house. And if they had, she would've found a way to get them out by now. Her slender fingers grazing the wall like a stethoscope on a chest. I pressed my sternum to the wall to make my heartbeat line up with theirs. But I couldn't hear anything over the mewing.

Jack tries to believe me but I know he doesn't. His doubt is like rocks I kick down the street. I bite the nails I still have while he explains that he wants to hear it too. I tell him he's not trying hard enough and that he's almost always asleep when it happens. We aren't arguing. But I get the sense that he thinks of this house as his. Later, while he slept, I waited for them. But there were no noises that night and I started to get worried. The hole was his idea. But all it accomplished was getting plaster all over our bed. I'm still picking it out of our hair like fleas. If he couldn't hear them, he felt sure he would be able to see them. But the drill broke. He never finished. I press my palm against it at night. I'm not sure if I still hear the mewing or if I'm just hearing what I used to stuck on repeat.

My mother never liked my boyfriend.

"Jack is going to take you away," she said. I knew she was right but I went anyway. When she calls her messages ask when I'm coming back. She doesn't think this will work out because he and I are different kinds of people. But that's what he says about her. Neither of them knows what they're talking about. I didn't take much with me and my mother wouldn't mail me anything. Some socks, one warm sweater, and all of my jeans. All the dresses she made are still hanging in my closet. She would never admit it, were it true, but sometimes I picture her running the blade of her finger over them. She and I moved slowly. Pouring coffee, cooking eggs, buying milk every week. I guess it was routine but it doesn't feel that way now, looking back.

I'm waiting for my other fingernails to fall like dead leaves. They're turning yellow and purple. The thumbnails already started to grow back. Clear and ugly. I can't feel anything with either of them. Or rather, everything feels like ice. Jack put my thumb in his mouth and said it tasted like kale. His tongue didn't taste like anything and when he ran it over my thumb again I looked away. There are these fleeting moments when I think my mom was right but those are the same moments that I'm best at tricking myself into loving him. My mother's shoulder blades are so pointed, like her elbows. All her bones seem dangerous, possibly lethal, probably harmless, like a sword made of sugar. Like those little kitten's claws. Not strong enough to dig through plaster. But Jack's bones and hands aren't strong enough either. Whatever is trapped won't be helped by either of them.

The sounds have grown more guttural. I think they're surviving by eating whatever insect life has made its home in there too. Termites or fleas or ants. Little white moths with hairy bodies and papery wings. Sometimes there are two praying mantises on our windowsill. When the kittens get out I wonder if they'll eat them too. Their bodies look like wind-up toys.

My boyfriend has taken to going for walks at night. He knows I've been staying up, waiting for the sounds, and he gets jealous. At night the hours are frantic like a lost child. It means something. That white space between words and between trees or people. I always think this. When we met he was my friend's boyfriend and asked me to dance at a bar. The whole time we moved I thought of her watching us and laughing. Drunk and happy.

My mother has cracked palms. Jack's hands are always clammy. He isn't subtle or good with words. But he's a great dancer. Though you wouldn't know it to look at him.

When he's out at night I hear noises that aren't the kittens. At first it was motorcycles and car brakes screeching like dying geese. I heard men laughing and the fire escape wincing. Now the noises are quiet. I have to press my ear to the window and strain to hear them. They seemed sinister until I felt the vibrations in my fingers and started to think it might be my throaty laugh or burning screech. But I know what's real and what isn't. I don't think our neighborhood is dangerous but it's not too smart to walk around at three in the morning. I can't sleep until he gets home or I hear the kittens. The sounds are so faint now.

A couple weeks after I first heard the sound Jack took a blue ballpoint pen and traced all the lines on my hands and fingers. He drew in nails where I had none. I took it and traced around the veins in his forearm. We looked like cartoons. His hands felt doughy and strange, like they were blistering under the skin where I couldn't see. We were too busy laughing at the blue ink to notice my mother pull up to our curb. She was holding a bag of basil. No one invited her. She didn't even invite herself. She turned the bag over spilling green leaves onto our kitchen table. The smell stuck to my hair. I rubbed a leaf on my wrist while she boiled water. She set a knife next to Jack on the floor and told him to get started.

"Where's she going to sleep?" Jack asked, knife floating above the basil. The couch cushions are nicer than our bed. And certainly cleaner. But she doesn't buy it and I can't sleep so far from the scratching. I watch Jack's chest rise and fall. I play his ribs like a piano and still he sleeps. My mother's face looks older with her eyes closed. Her hair, let loose from its braid forms a nest by her ear. I won't tell her about them. Not yet. She'll want to fix it and I'm not ready for them to go. The next morning I'm awake. Awake enough, but I want to get in my bed when she leaves it and sleep all day. And when I finally get up. When I'm up for good. I hope everyone is gone and the dry wall is cracked and the cats or whatever they are crawl out and start to chew on my fingers. I'll be still. I won't move at all.

"He isn't good for you." My mother hovers over my head, which is dangling off the arm of the couch. A blanket tangles around my legs.

"Where is he?" I ask.

"I sent him to the store. For chicken. There's no food here."

"We eat. It's just not always our first priority."

"That's what I mean." She walks back to the kitchen. I notice how thin her ankles are in their flat shoes. How her skin looks washed, like putting your underwear in the machine on the wrong setting. My hair is oily and limp; I don't move it out of my eyes when I walk to the bedroom to check on them. The hole Jack started has gotten bigger. There's a pile of plaster on the floor. It's dirty, like ashes. For days we were relegated to the couch while my mother cooked and made us clean and I still hadn't told her about the wall. I was starting to fear it was something bigger. Something that was meant to stay inside its narrow prison. At night I felt warm breathe on my neck that I was sure didn't belong to Jack. It made me crave real air, not the kind made from city heat and bodies too close to each other.

I would wake up to her braiding the ends of my hair.

At night, when we thought she was asleep, Jack and I would sit in the kitchen and eat peanut butter out of the jar. With our ankles locked and our knees touching, he told me not to go.

"She's been packing your things when we aren't around."

"No. She wouldn't do that."

"Then where did all of your tights go? You don't wear them anymore and they aren't in the underwear drawer." I don't have an answer for him. I had accepted their disappearance without question. If you think about it long enough you can make anything make sense. If she stays long enough, she might just get me to move back home. Jack licks peanut butter off my upper lip and we fall sleep for a while on the cold kitchen floor. When I wake up my jaw feels bruised and there are tile imprints on my arm. It's like someone turned a screw in my ear.

My mother wants all of the windows open all the time. It's getting cold and my face is chapped. I'm starting to think maybe Jack was right. Only instead of taking me home she is going to stay here until he leaves. I don't know where she goes during the day but she usually comes back with food and cooks without speaking. If she's trying to poison us she is failing. At night I press my nose into Jack's shoulder blade. I don't inhale. I just listen. *Don't leave,* I think. *I won't,* he thinks back.

The noises—all of them—get louder, but only for me. I can hear my mother's hair growing and Jack's ribs cracking. When she cuts peaches I can feel the knife hit the pit before it happens. It hurts my teeth. Jack goes for walks during the day now. I'm never alone. One of them is always in the next room or watching me sleep or trying to convince me I'm being fooled. I rarely go into my bedroom. The room, which has quickly become my mother's. But from the doorway I can see the wall cracking, the hole growing larger. If she has heard them she hasn't said so.

We dust every day, Jack and I. For her. And also because I need to get closer to the wall. To make sure it is just plaster and not something else. I check for small hairs and the soft pads of feet.

I notice my mother and Jack whispering when I walk in the room. Their hatred has melted down to mistrust. Of me. Of each other too. He told her about the kittens, I'm sure. And now she looks like she has a plan. I don't want a plan. I don't want sledgehammers and hospital masks. Jack still makes fun of her drawl but it's almost flirtatious. I vomit into the sink.

On an unseasonably hot afternoon my mother makes fried green tomatoes. We eat them with bacon and sourdough bread. At once, but not in unison, they tell me they're worried.

"I know you go into my room during the day and stare at the wall."

"It's okay, it's just, like, your thing," Jack says.

"No. It's strange. What are you looking at? Jack said you hear something."

"We should buy a new drill and finish the hole. Then we'll know for sure." I don't care if they believe me. And I don't want a drill. They have to find their own way out. I didn't understand before but I understand now. The wall won't break until they're ready.

Jack and I go for a walk and I tell him my new plan. He gets this look on his face that I've never seen before. Earnest. Something. His teeth look crooked. Or maybe they've always been that way. My plan isn't so much a plan as a step. A hint. We could accidentally kill them if we do it wrong using a drill or a sledgehammer. What I want doesn't have that risk. I don't care if my mother and Jack think I'm hallucinating. But I want her to leave. Maybe I can only think of her fondly when I miss her. He touches my short, stiff thumbnails. He brings them to his lips and I think he's mad. But really he's scared. *It's okay*, I think, *It will be over soon*. He whispers something in my ear but I can't understand what he's saying through my closed eyes.

I start with one. I use a thumbtack to nail it to the wall.

The dried apricots feel like the bottoms of my feet. My mother agrees to switch rooms. To try the couch just for these last few days before her departure. She hasn't said she's leaving, but what would be the point of her staying? I nailed them in a line, a curved one, running almost parallel to the largest crack. I'm hoping I'll be done with them before the flies and ants come. The room smells sickly sweet, like butterscotch mixed with half and half. I start another line. Halfway through it happens. Just below the hole Jack made a piece of plaster falls out. Not quite large enough for a child's fist to fit through. I keep nailing the apricots and can hear their breathing. It's so loud Jack and my mother can finally hear it. They paw at the wall behind the fruit. But they're too tiny to break it. What has all along sounded like one or two animals is at least half a dozen. I can't see them but I see their shadows moving.

Jack walks over and pulls more plaster away. He throws the apricots in and the sound of their teeth is so high pitched we have to plug our ears. My lungs are tight. My stomach too. Being proven right doesn't feel like I thought it would. They aren't birds, but there are damp feathers stuck in the plaster. Jack says they aren't like any kittens he's ever seen but he's wrong.

When we reached into the wall, my mother and I, what we pulled out was indeed mewing. It was pink and hairless with tiny translucent teeth and nails. They all were. My mother's stretched itself across her hands. The one I held touched his paws to his ears. Like being outside his drywall prison was shocking. Like the sound of the world, even in that silent bedroom, was making his skin peel backwards until he was nothing, just a noise, vibrating in my hands.

Weird

Christine DeSimone

Sunday streets splayed with pure, undiffused light
that bled from a hot blue sky, a dome
of heat that gave concrete a painful bite
and every distant surface a little glint of flame.

Church mornings in the uncool Olds,
our mother fuzzed the AM radio knob
to the Beatles hour. We were doled
only their early years—the dull doo-wop

of "Please Please Me," "Love Me Do," soap-scrubbed
harmonies of peppy English boys—while the pulse
of sun seared our seatbelt buckles. We begged:
Didn't they do any better songs than this?

But no—after '65, the Beatles "got weird,"
she sniffed. "I hope you kids never get
into that stuff." For the umpteenth time, she peered
in the rear-view, puckered lipstick, rubbed a wet

finger over white front teeth. She coughed
the car to a stop in the chapel parking lot, earliest
as usual to arrive, then slid from the soft
and sticky vinyl, pulling down the back of her dress.

Our Tongues Like Stars

Christopher J. Michel

The glum spectators of astronomy now / know the biggest whatsits in existence / are holes at the cores of galaxies, / each eating billions of stars. How tired

this makes me feel. I have a kitchen / floor to sweep & re-dirt / & sweep & it'll be one hundred / thousand years post-me before

the gods our generations fashion / to replace us reach another planet / capable of sentience. But I know / I'll roast an eggplant tonight. I will

blend it with oil & sunflower seeds. / My now thirteen-months daughter, / the smallest living object / in existence once, & the god I made

/ to replace me, will eat alongside me, / & someday she will make her own / meals for me. I'm teaching her

to sweep & eat & keep in mind / the larger whatsits of existence: / I sprinkle hot sauce on the dip, / to prickle our tongues like stars.

What the Arctic Ground Squirrel Dreams

Christopher Michel

The Arctic Ground Squirrel lies / beneath the tundra all but two months of the year, / temperature lower than ice, natural antifreeze / in its veins. But every other week it shivers / into warmth and for a night, it dreams. / I've never seen this. I read it from a journalist / who took what natural philosophers bore witness / to, and made a tale to illustrate his parables of wonder, / But I take on faith the words I read as true. As you / reader, must utilize some sum of your faith, too.

Reader, did you know about the Arctic / Ground Squirrel and its torpid state? Regardless, details / of the creature's fate must echo / the unsolved problems of our hearts. / Else why bother treading through / these words in quest of a frozen mammal's / roscid dreams? Better now to raise your head and ask / what images your own fortnightly kindled / inner life could manifest reflected in the slack synaptic / pulses of a shut-in's totem, buried under / winter tundra, conjuring impossible orange light / eternally setting over wet elysian fields, ripe / with bilberry, giant mushroom, willow roots; / the cool breeze bringing interesting smells; the fox / or owl outpaced by an easy burst of speed.

A Coda for Saint Anne

Ray Shea

Dusk smears tired blackface
across a Mardi Gras sky,
crusties and vampires conspire,
buskers wind down
and pass a bottle,
a drag queen loses her wig.

The Society of Saint Anne
came to the levee to remember,
brandishing crepe-ribboned hula-hoops
against the breeze,
before scattering back amongst the living,
their flags abandoned in the riprap
like the battle standards
of the kagemusha.

A lone beefeater
in Tudor red and gold
embroidery
steps unseen
past the drunks
and over the fallen
to the water's edge
to waft solemn gray dust
from a parade-worn sack.

Farewell to flesh,
ashes to sea
the river unchanged
like the Ship of Theseus
no matter how many dead
are replenished
into its current.

Mortuary Band on Stockton Street

~

Carina Yun

Even the children hush to silence.
The trumpet men play his name
as they ride through the streets.

They shout high from their horns
and croon from their chests.

We stare from the sidewalk,
stare into a widow's eyes as she
straightens her face, stare at his

picture as they parade.
We file like ants on the sidewalk,

our backs pressed against boxes
of dried fish and cabbage, our umbrellas
anchored carrying the weight.

We watch for the hand in the hearse
throwing spirit money into the rain.

Powell Street

~

Carina Yun

A homeless man begs
with a filthy Styrofoam cup.

A union strikes outside
Macy's with cardboard signs.

A toothless woman grabs
my wrist. She asks me for my

baby teeth. It is pouring ice
pellets in July. My mother

clutches my tiny hands
and skids down the street

pulling me. My hair dries
under her open coat.

An old man in a hospital
gown pushes a wheelchair

to the food bank, cigarette
butt hanging from the corner

of his mouth. He carts
five bags of stale bread,

while I stand in the meal line
with my mother, smelling

the stench of urine and think
of all-you-can-eat buffet.

In the soup kitchen, a girl
with disheveled hair

drops her brownie. Her
cries like a calf being weaned

from its mother.
I give her my brownie,

each bite as precious as
jade through shop windows.

A No Good Thunderstorm

Alexis Pope

Dear Hurricane, my name is gentle
release. My name is no, I will not drive
across the country to escape you.
I've named you after my mother-in-law
is how I feel this morning. Tea, because
the coffee tastes like salt. I won't find
you tomorrow under the bed, or out
my window on this cold April where you
hail onto my hair. I'm worried about the wind
blown, how to survive you. I wear this
hopeful, light jacket. Dear hurricane,
I'm afraid to leave you. Brush off my lap
with your heavy fingers. Offer myself
to the fish. Where I find you is out back
on a depressed swing set. We lie
to ourselves about summer. A barefoot
expectation while we wait it out. I ordered
this pizza for you, crafted this birthday
hat, bought the streamers & this banner
& expected something like death
in return. At least something that means
you care enough to hurt me. Float
through me like you mean it, that's what
this is about. Eat this cake like you're
starving, that's what I want. Wash over me
like a hurricane. I need something
more than clean.

Crabmeat on the Fifteenth Floor

James Norcliffe

The platters circulate
the terrace, the proffered
legs carapaced in red

with flesh protruding
white, wet with the scent
of the ocean, of sex.

This should be forever:
as if forever tasted
of Riesling and crabmeat,

as if forever lingered
on your fingers long
after the door closed,

long after the elevator
slid silently down
to the brilliant lobby.

Ivan Albright

David Dodd Lee

I live in a certain unburnished Aristotelian centrum of light

my copper brothers in prison

This might explain the barbed-wire hotel rooms   the invisible owls

Here, right here, I am a smiling Hat

and with such finely trimmed nails

a basket of laundry for a head . . .

And this button   if I push it hard enough the stars come on

It's the taproot of night   the trees are throbbing

He divided each feather into a thousand such paintbrushes—

multiplication of faces into islands of age

even the dust motes felt rage

You can purport to need such endless devotion

laughing, like a weather vane all lit up

pointing East
pointing West

The ribs of a whale are burning at the edge of the sea

School

~

Hinemoana Baker

And now it's the Gay Gordons, my feet a
cold, dead, empty place, my enemies a
parliament of owls, all palms but mine bone-
dry, mouth full of sky and counting. Buildlings

make their tartan way down green hillsides, my tights
are too low in the crutch, but oh the ribbed
grey velvet of them is just right. Needless
to say I'm wearing Tee-bars, black, but not

even the left one's perfect scuffed upper,
curling overstrap, buckle freckled with
rust can keep me safe from the evil pre-
ordainment, devil choreography

no orientation day with a red
cliptop box of luncheon sausage
sandwiches, a feijoa and a box
of raisins can prepare you for.

Altitude (for Madeline)

Hinemoana Baker

It's patchouli, isn't it, that you wear?
When you walk it's praise to the deity
of Dykedom and James Dean, *a viola*
you remind me in your email.
Kuan Yin couldn't lean that sexy
and wise on the roof of a Nissan
Sentra. What can I say to empty
the coma from you? Justice and
neurosis are lung disorders, too.
I won't put you crook. Strangle your worries.
Remember you're at altitude.
There's a spoonbill and a harbour
the colour of aotea. There's a white heron.

Pinocchio's Heart of Darkness

Meghan Tifft

It was Halloween night and I was at the grocery store. I couldn't exactly remember getting there. It seemed to me like I had just appeared suddenly, out of some airless void of blackness. There were the empty checkout lines, the extinguished Lotto sign, the wall of cigarettes. It was too soon for the pills to be working—I took them right before I left the park. We were playing baseball, or maybe we had stopped playing. My friends were all shouting names at me when I left. Was that why I left? I couldn't remember. Sometimes it just felt good to walk away from those assholes.

So I knew what I wanted. Chocolate milk and peanuts—unshelled nuts because I liked to use the scoop. I used to work the all-night shift at a place like this in Miami, and I couldn't help feeling something familiar as I wandered into the steady fluorescent hum. It was like being stranded on a moon in another galaxy. Stuck in a bottle of revolving light. I still hadn't seen anybody yet. It was beginning to feel eerie, like I was dreaming again. Or maybe the pills were working. Then I turned the corner and saw a clerk leaning over a bin at the back. As I got closer I saw he was covering the potatoes with a big gray blanket. I had to wonder about that. Like he was putting them to bed.

"Goodnight Mom," I said, and he startled like a pony. I felt a soft cloudy wave of laughter pass through me.

"Oh. You scared me," he said.

"Happy Halloween."

He smiled. He had a gap between his two front teeth and a sparse, chewed up beard. When I looked at him I felt a slow simmering warmth rise up in my chest, and I didn't know why.

"Nice costume," he said.

"Ha ha."

"So what are you supposed to be?"

I jingled the change in my pockets. "You can't tell?" I was wearing a red felt hat that someone had pulled from a hall closet earlier in the night with a feather sticking out of it. I lifted my eyebrows, waiting for his guess, and that was when I understood the feeling from before. I tried not to smile. "I'm Kenny the grocery clerk," I said.

He looked like he was waiting for me to make sense. It was amusing. I had always liked to see him squirm, all the way back to middle school. But there was something else about that look too. I knew what it was. I had a girlfriend who used to look at me exactly that way—blue eyes pinning light—whenever she got mad at me.

"Wait," Kenny said, and he cracked a timid smile. "Do I know you?"

"I don't think so. I read your nametag."

I watched him look down to make sure it was there, but it was underneath his apron where I couldn't see it.

I smiled. "Just here for some nuts," I told him.

I'm good at playing dumb. My ex-girlfriend used to say that to me and not in a complimentary way. She said a lot of things that weren't very nice and then of course I said things back that were equally unkind. It seemed like this went on the whole summer we lived together, the fighting back and forth, like a game we started one night and couldn't stop playing.

"What's wrong with you?" she said one time. "You get off on this too much."

"Really? Is that what he said to you?" I asked, meaning her previous boyfriend.

He used to hit her, and once I heard the stories I couldn't separate her from him, not even when I touched her, like she still carried the imprint of his fists on her body. She was delicate, one of those pale, moonstruck girls whose limbs were all silver and milk light, and she was twitchy too. She didn't like to have the lights on in the bedroom when she was getting undressed. I had walked in on her more than once like that and she'd always shrivel up in front of me, like a spider I'd startled in the sink at night. In those moments I felt like the attacker. I didn't want to scare her. But for some reason, looking at her like that, I could see how he had hit her.

I used to walk away and imagine myself doing what he had done, and it was like imagining my own death, all that airless panic welling up inside me. I had dreams about running into him in public somewhere, this person whose face I'd never seen. He still called her sometimes. I used to have to go outside while she talked to him. Even now I couldn't think about it without feeling electric, like a light bulb sizzling out. I had to shake it off physically, with a roll of my head and a shrug of my shoulders. I reached out and picked up the metal scoop, cold brushed aluminum, dusty with flaking peanut skin. I held it up in front of Kenny. "Do you like nuts?" I asked.

He didn't answer. His eyes were really scouring me now, moving over my nose and down to my chin where I could feel the tight heat of the scab that hadn't healed yet. I was surprised he didn't recognize me. Did I look that different? My hair was longer and my nose was a wreck, more like a pipe welded to my face than a real nose, but still.

"It's not that bad," I said.

"What?"

I shrugged and dug the scoop in. I felt the dry shift and tumble of the nuts and smelled the earth and the dust. I tried to remember what we had been talking about. My palm was damp and the metal handle was cold, and I felt a long deep shiver snag somewhere inside me and pull its way through until I felt like I had turned inside out. "Shit," I said, and let the handle drop. I looked at Kenny. He had turned away to finish his tasks at the bin and I was looking at the blank hump of his back. I tied my bag of peanuts looking around the produce area. "So," I said. "This is all yours is it?"

Kenny glanced back at me over his shoulder. He frowned. He seemed disappointed I was still here. "Well—it's not *mine*."

I felt a surge of that old annoyance. Good old Kenny. "But you're in *charge* of all this produce," I told him. "You take care of it." I gestured to his blanketed potatoes. "You're the mama. The bitch of this litter."

Kenny pushed his glasses up. He cast a nervous glance away from me, into the store. There was a wedding ring on his finger. "Yes I work in produce, if that's what you mean," he said.

"That's quite a responsibility," I told him. "There's a lot here. A real bounty." I gestured grandly and let my hand drop into a bin of purple onions. I kept looking at the wedding ring. It was big and silver. White gold. Idly my hand cupped an onion and flicked it out. I watched it hit the bin of potatoes and fall with a dreary thump. A thick sound. A fist on flesh.

"Why did you do that?" Kenny said.

"It was an accident." Those were her words too. She had said them to me the first time we met. "She lied," I said, and then I picked the onion up. I looked at it in my hand and then at Kenny. "This is an onion," I said, showing it to him, "not a girl." I put the onion back.

Kenny was silent. I could see his thoughts rapidly clicking behind his eyes as he wondered when this was going to turn into a joke on him. Was it going to? I gazed around at all the colored piles and pyramids around us and felt like laughing. Maybe I was waiting for the joke too.

"So," I said, "how much of this rots before it sells?"

Kenny gave a little smile, not a friendly one, and said, "You'd be surprised, actually."

"Oh really? Where does it all go—in the trash?" I knew where it went. I worked in one of these places before.

"Well no." Kenny hesitated and pointed to the black double doors. "First it goes back there."

I looked at the doors. I saw their two round, dark windows and felt them pull at me like deep space. "Can I see?"

"I'm really not supposed to do that."

I could picture it in my mind, the big sagging box full of all those moldering fruits and vegetables. "Well—what if I wanted to buy something?" I said, wondering where I was going with this. "Would you sell it half price?"

He sighed.

I felt a little sorry for him but now I couldn't help myself. I leaned in and said in a soft woozy voice like I was confiding in him, "I don't have much money."

His eyes darted away from mine and then settled somewhere over my head. "Oh," he said. "Well I don't—"

"Come on. Would you ever give something away if it was bad

enough? Instead of throwing it out?"

Kenny sucked air in through his teeth. There was a look of pain on his face as he stared in the direction of the double doors, trying to make up his mind. "Well, let me just go see what's back there," he said finally, putting his big red palm out to block me. "Just stay here a minute."

Disappointed that I couldn't follow, I waited until the doors were swinging behind him and I could picture him digging through the rotten bin of fruit, all those dented soft bodies lying against each other, and then I walked away from the produce section into the store. A guilty pleasure sparked far down in my stomach and I tried to stoke it, smiling to myself as I walked, but I felt it sputter and die before I had reached the freezer section. I wondered why. In high school it would have amused me. In high school it was easy to be amused when it came to Kenny. I remembered what we used to do to him. At football games he would stand up on a pedestal in a white polyester suit and poke at the air with his wand. My friends and I would walk up to the back of the stands at halftime, ammo cradled in our shirts, rocks big enough to throw that far, and pretend to watch the band fan out over the field. It was our own game. There was one night I threw a rock and hit his cap, hard enough to knock it sideways, and afterwards I went out to the parking lot with my friends and shattered his windshield with a baseball bat.

We all sat in the bushes to watch him come out. When he did, he was still flushed from the game, looking satisfied about something, like victory was his. It was embarrassing. Who did he think he was? All he did was push the band around with his wand. He didn't win anything. When he reached his car and saw what I had done his face emptied into a look that was almost blind, like he was trying to see into a long and painful blackness. For a moment behind the bushes I felt like I was falling into that same blackness with him. I was thirty feet away and I felt heavy and stunned. Even the memory of it made me want to turn around, afraid he was right behind me. He wasn't though. It was just a long bright emptiness going back to the other side of the store. I turned around and walked along, my eyes squinted against the slick glare of the tiles. I felt more like I was gliding than walking. In the aisles a few late night shoppers were bent over their carts and staring ahead like zombies.

Halloween, I thought, and I felt another smile break across my face. I turned up the medicine aisle toward the refrigerators and a woman with long unwashed hair glanced up quickly and then looked away.

"Excuse me," I said, stopping in the middle of the aisle and reaching around her for a bottle of Robitussin.

"Oh," she said. Her eyes were a slick of wet brown mud, rolling down my face and over my nose and stopping at my chin.

"What, this?" I said, pointing at the scab from my fight in Miami. I mean fall. "Yeah really. It's nothing," I told her.

She looked away and didn't say anything.

"Don't worry about me," I said. "I know you don't care."

"You're not supposed to do that," she told me.

"Do what? My girlfriend didn't care either." I felt the plastic in my hand. I squeezed it and it gave a sharp crackle. I put the wrapper on the shelf where the bottle had been. "Hey," I said, leaning towards her. "I'm single and ready to mingle."

She gave me a look of disgust that made me feel strangely elated. "You don't have to look at me like that." I tried not to laugh as I peered into her cold, briny eyes. "My girlfriend was prettier than you." That last comment was an accident. It was the eyes that made me say it. I couldn't help myself. I could see them in my mind, bowls of deep blue light, still and miraculous. "I'm sorry," I said. I wasn't sure who I was talking to. The last time I had seen my girlfriend's eyes, they were flushed pink as a sunset. She was angry. She was crying.

"It's your fault," she said to me.

"Okay." I remember saying that. "Well I guess I should have beat you shitless. I guess I should have held lit matches to your hair. I guess I should have squeezed bruises into your arms and thrown boiling water on your feet. Then maybe you'd like me better." That wasn't what I meant to say, but I was angry. I don't know what I meant to say.

"Fuck you," she said, her voice suddenly cold and remote, an arctic wind blowing on a winter planet. "You're fucked up."

"No," I said. "He's the one that's fucked up." Then I said, "You two deserve each other." I said this because I knew where she was going. And she didn't contradict me. She just looked at me with those blue eyes, telling me everything and nothing at once.

The girl in the aisle had turned her back on me and now I watched her drifting further away. "Hey—where you going? Was it something I said?" I called out. She cast a furtive glance back before she turned the corner, and I waved. Then I turned and walked in the other direction, smiling at the medicines as I went.

At the end of the aisle I glanced in either direction to see if anybody was watching and took four fast burning gulps out of the bottle of Robitussin. I finished the bottle in two more gulps and took a deep ragged breath. I cleared the heavy bitter mucus out of my throat, then bent over between the eggs and a low open freezer and hacked quietly until my throat was raw. At least I hoped I was quiet. A few strings of cherry red drool stretched from my mouth into a little pool on the floor and I smeared it away with my foot. It reminded me of the time I bent over and spit blood into the grass after the fight. That wasn't very long ago, I reminded myself. And it wasn't a fight. I let these thoughts drift away again under the soft gnashing inside my head, wondering how long it would be before I was seeing the world in Technicolor visions. In high school, my best friend drank a bottle of Robitussin and said he had those visions. But he was always saying stuff like that.

"He was an asshole," I said out loud, and startled myself. He was still an asshole. I had left him down at the park, calling out names after me as I walked away. Slurs and insults he'd been using since high school. It was pathetic, how little had changed. When I left for Miami, my friends were working dead-end jobs and getting drunk every weekend night at the batting cages. When I came back, all I had to do was walk down to the park, and there they were. I remember the little party we made of my homecoming, how everybody pitched in for something and then we rotated through the cages until we didn't know one end of the bat from the other. I'd be lying if I said it didn't feel good, swinging that bat. It was the first right feeling I'd had in a long time. I swung and it was like there were two broken parts of me, one holding the other, finally coming into perfect contact. I almost expected to see sparks fly up into the night, showering out a victory signal for me. But then I told myself there was no victory. I hadn't won anything. I hadn't even done anything. I was supposed to be the smart one, the one who got out. And all I'd done was end up back here.

I straightened up and wiped my mouth on my shirt, feeling strange. I was looking down into the freezer bin, at the thick icy banks hugging the big tubs of ice cream down below. I could feel an urge coming on. There was no one around. "Don't eat the yellow snow," I said to no one in particular. The burst of cold air felt good. Then I leaned forward and aimed a steady yellow stream into the freezer. First I went for the ice crystals, melting them down to slush. Then I made pools and splatters on the lids of the ice cream tubs. When I was done I paused, waiting out that last drip, and I saw myself down there perched over the frosty hair of the freezer, like a brown mouse looking out over the edge of a lonely iceberg. It didn't seem very funny. I glanced up, wondering what would happen if somebody caught me. I thought of Kenny on the other side of the store. What would he say if he saw what I was doing? And before I could help it the empty look of violation on his face came floating up into my mind. The one I had seen so many times before. When I saw it I almost felt panic, at a great and sentimental distance. It was a sad and beautiful feeling, and I stepped back from the freezer with a shiver that seemed like a kind of amazement.

It was time to leave. It was time to get out of here. To get back to the park. I reached down and closed my zipper. Then I remembered my chocolate milk. A warm gluey thickness was spreading down into my limbs and I had some trouble getting into the refrigerator. Eventually I pulled out one of the bottles and let the door fall closed. I turned around and went down the nearest aisle toward the front of the store. I had this feeling though. Why was there all this cloth around my heart? For a moment I thought I was about to see something. A splattering of bright lacquered plastic materialized out of the blur of my gaze and I looked over at a tumble of gleaming orange spheres. A mound of rainbow wigs spilling out onto the floor. A slack rubber mask with bulging red eyeballs. The holiday aisle. I almost forgot—it was Halloween. Then just to amuse myself I tilted my head back and gave out a loud, sinister Dracula laugh.

I thought of the few shoppers in the other aisles, looking up at the maniacal sound and furrowing their brows. But nobody peered anxiously down my aisle, no manager asked me to take my mischief outdoors. There was just a slick, greasy quiet when I had finished. I shrugged, and then I felt stupid. What was I doing here? The night seemed to stretch away from me like it would reach out into eternity. How long had I been standing here? What time was it?

A voice jabbed into my ears like a hot poker and I winced. I turned and looked at the two indistinct shapes that had been hovering in my periphery.

"It's 1:15," said one of them, as if I had asked her something. "Cute. You're Pinocchio."

I gave her an ugly sneer, not on purpose, and tried to breathe. "Halloween's over," I said.

"Okay. There's no need to be a downer. The candy's not half off yet."

I looked her over. I could see the red bodysuit and her long black ponytail trailing down over her shoulder like tar. "You're the devil," I told her.

She smiled with long teeth. "Well, usually," she said. "But tonight I'm in disguise."

The hefty one with the cat ears smiled meekly into her neck.

"I get it." I already knew which one I liked and which one I didn't. But that didn't mean I wasn't going to try. "So what are you then?"

"A Red Hot."

A picture of a red hot formed in my mind, shiny and round. "She should be the red hot." I saw my finger pointing and wished I hadn't said that. She would either think I was calling her hot or fat, when actually she was neither. "I was joking," I said, and then felt their nervous laughter falling over me like bright, scattering coins. "Why don't you be quiet?" I asked.

"You're not very nice Pinocchio," said the devil. But I could tell she was into me. Her friend could too. I saw her eyes dart between us like she didn't know which of us she trusted less. Without the little bit of padding she would have been the pretty one.

"I'm very nice," I said, focusing my gaze on the devil. Her upper lip seemed to be snagged on her teeth. "Just wait until we're alone together."

"Don't hold your breath."

I could see she was holding hers, so I said, "I have an idea. Why don't we all go to the park down the street and play baseball."

"Baseball?" said the cat.

"My friends are there. We have a keg. And whatever else."

The devil turned to her friend. "You want to?" she said.

I saw the cat look down at her big rubber watch.

"He's not getting off for another forty-five minutes," said the devil.

"Who?"

The cat seemed to give me a small embarrassed smile. She looked back at the devil. It was pretty sweet, the way she smiled at me. I stared at them a moment longer, wondering if I had lost track of something. They were talking quietly between themselves, excluding me from their conversation. I saw the devil shrug and the cat ask her a question I couldn't hear, and then I wondered why I was staring at them. They would notice me in a second and it would be embarrassing. I started to walk away down the aisle and behind me I heard the cat groan. It seemed to take a long time to get to the checkout line. I kept walking toward the puff of light that marked the last register at the end of the row. Somewhere in that time I forgot that I wasn't alone, and then remembered again when one of them said, "Hey. Aren't you going to pay?"

"What?" I said. I passed the checkout line and kept going past a bin of apples in front of the big glass doors. Then I went right through them without looking back.

"You didn't pay for that," said the cat when we were outside. I was moving slowly through blurry waves of air, concentrating hard on getting to the sidewalk at the edge of the parking lot.

"It was an accident," I said.

"No. I think you did it on purpose."

"What?" I had been going slow and now I stopped. I felt strange, like an animal in the beam of somebody's flashlight. Her hot voice was ringing in my ears.

"What happened to your face?" said the devil. "Did you get in a fight?"

“I fell,” I said. But the hat was cutting loud streams of air over my ears and I couldn’t hear myself anymore. I stared hard at the faces that were shivering in front of me. “Am I talking?” I said. “It was an accident,” I said again. I lifted my fingers to my face and felt a streak of pain shoot out across my nose. “I think I broke it.” The wind was gushing past my ears and I couldn’t think. It sounded like leaves rushing together. It was like water, filling my ears. Like when I opened the car door that day and stepped out. There were the blue shadows on the street, soft and swaying. I looked up the concrete walkway to the wide sagging porch and there she was, eating an ice cream cone and talking on the phone.

“Tell him to come out,” I said. I was going to fight him.

“He’s not here,” she told me.

“Bullshit.”

She shrugged. “Go inside if you want.”

I went in, my heart beating wildly. I had driven fast all the way there just so I would feel reckless and cruel, but now I could feel all my conviction draining away like I had an open vein. There was the couch where he had pulled her hair and snapped her head back against the wall. It was light gray, with flat pillows.

“What?” she said, when I came back outside.

It was my last chance. “Why did you come back here?”

She cocked her head like this was an interesting question. Her hair was pulled back and her face looked pale and blue in the dusk. “Why? Does it bother you?”

“Listen,” I said. Of course it did. Of course it bothered me. “I wanted to ask you something.”

“Are you drunk?” she asked. “You’re on something, aren’t you?”

“What are you doing here?” I said. “Are you staying?” I hadn’t meant to ask so many questions. I kept looking away from her at the screen door as if it could help me put my thoughts in better order. All I could think was that she didn’t need this. I was better than this. I had come here to prove it, and to get rid of him once and for all. But now he wasn’t there and I felt like a broken toy that couldn’t do anything, couldn’t even open my mouth to talk to her. I felt my legs moving on the porch, stiff and numb, and everything I couldn’t say filling my throat like a hard wooden fist.

"Wait a second," she said. "You're leaving?"

"No," I said. But I kept walking.

"Okay that's nice. You should never have come here," she said before I had made up my mind. She stood up and I had an urge to make her sit down again. "It's a lucky thing he wasn't here." She opened the screen door and I felt it batter shut behind her. At some point my foot tried to find the first step and came down on air instead. For an instant I saw the blind panel of sidewalk tilting up toward my face and then the wind rushing out of the yellow leaves and curling swiftly over me like the lid of an eye closing shut.

I waited for the end of the fall but it never came. Instead I felt myself swaying like I was on the end of some string just before it broke, and I realized I was looking out through black static into the dim yellow lights of the parking lot.

"Hey!" said a voice behind me. I turned and saw somebody move in front of the light from the doors. "You took that. I saw you!"

"Stay back," I called out in a raw voice. "Leave her alone."

"What's Pinocchio's problem?"

"Are you okay? Do you need to sit down?" That wasn't what she said before. I thought this as I watched his heavy apron ripple out with every stride. Then I stepped in front of her.

"Hey," he said loudly, and I felt my hand circling something, a pale handle of flesh, sturdy and soft.

"Stop," she said. "What are you doing?"

His arm snapped through the air like he had just pitched a baseball. A heavy clot of pain erupted on my chest and I looked down to see an apple roll out at my feet. For a moment I thought my own heart had fallen out of me.

"Ow," I said automatically, but it hardly felt that way. A pleasant heat was spreading out from the center of my chest and radiating through me. It was like a bright spark of sunlight alighting in the middle of a cold and tranquil blackness.

"Get away from her," he said, and now he was right in front of me. Close.

"Don't," she said, and I squeezed harder.

I watched him drop his shoulder and put his foot back, ready for a fight, and now I knew how it must have felt to be her, like he was about to reach down into me and extinguish what was there. "Let go," he said.

But I couldn't move. I closed my eyes and waited for his fist to come streaking forward with crashing heat, to send my body reeling back into the night once and for all. There was something in my hand, warm and squirming and trying to get loose.

"Let go," he said.

But I couldn't. I couldn't let go.

Frozen Limbs

Kate Scarpetta

for Adrienne Rich

"We weren't even actually dating."

"So what? Emotionally, you were tethered. For years."

"So, why is it this dramatic? I feel like I've been stabbed."

"I don't see any blood, but I mean the chord's been cut. Look! You're here."

My friend, Jamie, smacks the hardwood floor through my yoga mat before squeezing my hand.

"I'm here but I'm not here."

Jamie's patience wears to nothing, and I realize why she does yoga.

"Well, where the fuck else are you? Stop driving in reverse and be here."

She smacks the mat again like a wrestler tapping out. This must be her visceral move of the evening. Donkey Konging all over my mat. My space is being encroached upon by everyone walking through the door of this place. How many can we fit in this poorly painted room? Walls with streaks in bright colors. All matte finishes even though this palette is ridiculous. I can imagine the trip to Home Depot by the owners. I know they said focal point more than once: "This gold will be a focal point."

Actually, the streak in that wall, because the primer wasn't properly done, is the "real" focal point. My *drishti*, where my gaze is going to be in "Tree Pose," will be that streak. Mark, set. It's getting really crowded in here. Can they turn someone away? "Sorry, no flow for you. Not tonight. You's late."

The instructor arrives. He looks all sage like. He's got a beaded prayer necklace draped over a shirt with Sanskrit running across it. "I made salt with Gandhi." That's totally what his Sanskrit says. He's got tattoos, more Sanskrit. Shit's everywhere, even his neck. Everyone in this class except me seems to be inked up and already halfway to removing their shirts. The Buddha man speaks:

"Alright, I can feel the energy tonight. Everyone come to the front of your mats in a seated position."

I'm here already. Half-lotus, because full-lotus is just too much. Some parts of yoga are just too much.

"Make this practice for the person next to you. Make this about being connected to one another."

Funny. You're funny yoga man. I came here to disconnect. To stop being attached. You're funny, man.

"Deep inhale."

My eyes close and I attempt to inflate my head. Suicide attempt number uno.

"On the exhale don't be afraid to be audible. Being 'audible' in your practice—in your life—is the most honest."

Some parts of yoga are just too much. Yet again, his sage zingers are making me shake my head. I was too audible at the bar last night. I was too audible when I found myself unable to say a sentence without dropping an F-bomb. I was honest and audible and completely embarrassing. The audible honesty killed my shot at a partner. At a shared life. Now I'm going to hold my breath. I'm going to explode right here next to the person I'm dedicating the practice to. She's a fine specimen, but I'm sure she can smell how negative I am. It's leaking out of my pores, and I haven't even begun to sweat yet. When I do, the whole class will know. They'll kick me out and be grateful that they'll have more room for inversions later.

The first *vinyasa* is so forced; it feels like my limbs are being guided by jerking strings from the ceiling, but by my fifth down dog, I'm feeling a little better. This girl, who I can't seem to stop thinking about, breaks through my layers of defense mechanisms with infuriating ease, like a flick of the wrist destroying a spider web. My heart is the juicy victim, falling then being caught in her waiting palm—only to have its legs torn off, one by one for the sport of it. Plucked and off balance. Thinking about this almost causes me to fall over when I jump back to a standing position from down-dog. Four *vinyasas* later, marks the completion of sun salutation A.," and with it, the spider image dissolves. Maintaining balance in tree pose feels good. It makes me not think about what I can't remember I said. Look at my leaves. Sway, delicate tree. For the first time since I woke up, I feel like I'm beautiful.

In warrior two, I start to feel energy. Charged sexuality. Maybe it's the sweat or maybe it's the heat. The room is steaming with this flow. I'm on the same page as the yoga guy now. We've reconciled and he doesn't even know it. I'm zenned the fuck out. Thinking about going to Bali. Skipping Christmas and living in a hut. Not shaving. I won't go that far. I'll shave, but I'll turn into someone like the woman next to me. I hope she couldn't smell the initial negativity. I hope she thinks I'm hot in that weird way. Her way. Her sexiness is palpable. Spank me, sap princess. She started with her shirt off. How fine is that?

"Warrior two, other side."

I turn, and now I get to stare at her back. There's a tattoo of text covering most of it. I don't speak the language it's in. I don't want to. I'd rather her whisper it to me after we've rolled around a bit.

"Swan dive, jump back, exhale into *chaturanga*, and inhale into *urdva mukha*. Five breaths."

Dive. Deeper into this positive escape. This sweet wonder of a tattoo goddess who is taking me on a journey out of my darkness.

"Bring yourself to child's pose and prepare for backbends. Your choice."

How yoga of him. To let us set some limits late in the game. But I'm high now. I'm up and wanting to show off. So, it's "camel" for me and my goddess. Hands in prayer while kneeling. I think of Madonna. I think of how the song, "Like a Prayer," is really about going down on someone. It's nothing like a prayer. I peak at my girl. She's already on her way back to this position that only true yogis and yours truly can do. I have always been able to hyperextend absurdly well. It's good for bed tricks. It's good for the end of yoga class. I think back to the lyrics. "Her voice will take me there." It really could. I extend my hands upwards. This is my pose. I smile and float back into an arch that's so unnatural and awesome, I can feel the instructor's eyes on me.

"Beautiful."

I don't have to look, but I know the instructor has made his way over. His bare, callused feet are planted on the hardwood next to me, in that four-inch space between Jamie's mat and mine. I can see his shower-worn hemp ankle bracelet out of the corner of my eye. It's been many moons since I've seen one of those bad boys. He feels my back to pretend to support it. I know he just wants to touch me. I know he is thinking that the girl and I could make a really sick pair. Just think of how well we'd fit together given this ability we share. Just think. I move into "full bow"—right from "camel" like it's nothing. It's something. I know it and so does guru.

"Yes. Beautiful."

Maybe we can have a three way. He's really into us. We're like a synchronized porno. If I were ever going to "minage-eh-twa," it'd have to have a male yoga instructor as the third. Otherwise, I'd feel a little cheap. Used. My breath is strong now. A force. On the inhale, I walk my hands toward my feet and come to a powerful mountain pose. Dude is right in front of my mat. He smiles. How can he resist?

I hate fish pose so much that it almost wrecks my jam. He saves my collapse with another child's pose. I'm overcome with gratitude. I think of my gifts: my family, the use of my limbs, the time I have to figure it out. I'll be ok. My body is warm. Comfortable here. Calmer. I reach. I extend forward and breathe with hope.

"Time for inversions. If there is more than a five percent doubt you'll fall into someone, please use a wall."

The mat is slippery. My first irritant is this ugly fact. No mat has ever been able to handle the amount I sweat. But, it's "headstand," and I've totally got this. Ponytail adjusted, and by the time I retie, goddess is already up like an inverted sphinx. What did Twain say about seeing the Sphinx? What word did he use? "Sentient." Yes. My fingers interlock, I drop my head into my palms, and I feel the weight shift to my forearms as I tip toe forward, waiting for the pendulum moment. My pelvis missed this feeling. This controlled and dignified act of balancing fear. I'm up. I'm breathing steady and pointing my toes like Gabby Fucking Douglas. Exhale down to inches. Then, slowly back up. Control. I'm in control again. The suddenness of it. It makes my skin hot. I come down, ready to be a corpse. Sentient.

Lying on my back, eyes closed. I take these moments to remember my friend next to me. Jamie brought me here to help because she knew that listening to me rehash what I can't remember wouldn't do anything. I had nothing to say. I just had to find a way to move, even this slowly. Even in place. "You just need to move," she said as she paid for my class. The yoga man beckons us back to life.

"In your own time, begin to come back to a seated position. We will end the class with three *Oms*."

I exhale. I try really hard to be into this.

"This is for the person next to you," he says.

I open my mouth and even though I'm not the best in the vocal arena, I *Om* for the goddess. I hold it as deeply as I can. As much as I try, I feel calmness slipping away. She's probably straight.

"This is for a person you are grateful for."

My mother. I should call her. She worries. She wants me to be happy, but I seem deficient. My calmness is tugged further. Toward the steamed windowpane of the studio. The coldness in the street. I want the ceiling to collapse. I want peace. *Om Shanti*, I believe, is how you say that.

"Last, for someone you hate. *Dvesha*."

I make no sound. Damn you, yoga man. I'm in no mood to *Om*. If I open my mouth, I'll scream. I want to cry but the anger in my ribcage suppresses the desire. It clings to my insides like steel-cut oatmeal. I'd faint if I let any more water come out of my body. I close my eyes. Coincidence. *Dvesha*. If anyone knew my *dvesha*, they would never ask me to Om about it. They'd accept that I'm just moving for now, and isn't that brave enough? *Namaste*, bitches.

Outside, it feels like there is a frigid puddle between my layers of clothes: two scarves, a long sleeve shirt, which capillary action had caused my sweat to dampen, and my winter coat, an impulse buy of puffy down. This must be what turtles feel like; thick shell with a disgusting, moist core. I wave goodbye to Jamie, who's headed back to her fiancé and French bulldog, in the East Village. I head into the The Mud Man, a coffee shop next door to the yoga studio. Half a cinnamon scone and one shot of espresso later has me penning a note to my sort-of-ex on a napkin, which, mind you, was made with 45% post-consumer recycled paper. Last night, my aggressive and bellig. display, fueled by three Belvederes and two shots of Jose, basically sealed the deal on me coming off as completely psychotic. It ended with her girlfriend grabbing her arm and escorting her out of the bar. My note isn't exactly "Keats," but it is honest. Audible honesty. Isn't that what I'm supposed to be shooting for now?

"I'm sorry. I love you. It looked like I was still a mess, but I swear I'm not."

I underlined "I'm not" and the napkin rips. A layered wound. I buy a stamp off an older woman, who I could just tell had one. The purse gave it away: muted *Vera Bradley* paisley nonsense. She was actually in the yoga class, but in the back row, because she is "new to yoga and an old lady who can't bend like you young girls anymore." I thank Trudy for the stamp and push through the heavy glass door.

The moment merits a cigarette. I'm down to two a week. This is my second, and it's only Sunday. Whatever. I see the mailbox on the end of the block and walk toward it quickly. I arrive, pull on the cold handle, reach into the pocket of my coat, and realize that I don't have an envelope. Damn it. My iPhone finds a stationary shop three streets over that is called, "Ink Panda." Weird name.

I give a weak wave at the owner, a blonde woman in her 40s who's wearing a crocheted sweater vest and impressively ugly loafers. She might be gay. My entrance to the shop is set to the music of soft bongo-esque clatter from a bamboo wind ornament clumsily attached to the door. More of these beauties are for sale and hanging above the handcrafted Papyrus birthday cards in the back right corner of the store. The lady is hard at work on an impressive round table display of St. Patrick's Day cards positioned amongst scattered gold-foiled chocolate coins that are spilling out of a black plastic cauldron. She offers me a coin and winks—she's totally gay—and I accept the candy currency even though I don't eat chocolate. Maybe I'll send it with my note. My girl does have a sweet tooth, which I find quite endearing.

I knew this place was going to be over the top expensive. I check out the apology cards. Most of them have cute animals on the front wincing or smiling like guilty school children. Most of them are also $7.00 or more. No fucking way am I paying for one of these. I grab a mint green card that goes with a kitten moping in a wicker basket. I hate cats. I peek at the woman, who is now whistling "Defying Gravity" from *Wicked*, while adjusting the arms of a creepy-ass leprechaun doll that sings "Macnamara's Band" when someone passes. The coast is clear, so I put the envelope in my pocket. I walk to the door, make it past the display, activating the stupid leprechaun, and my arm is grabbed.

"What do you think you're doing!'

Stealing an envelope. Duh.

"I saw that. I'll have you know that the proceeds of these cards help raise money for endangered pandas."

I suppress my laugh but can't help my eyebrows from mocking her statement. In a low tone, dripping with acid and the gaze of a teenager, I say, "Can't argue with that."

I walk back to the aisle and pick out a card with a penguin shrugging on it, as if to say "my bad" or "I don't know why I did that." I check out for my $6.20 card that is supposedly going to finance sexy time for Ling Ling and Ping Pong. As my debit card is being swiped, I read the mission statement scotch-taped to the counter. It informs me that Ling Ling and Ping Pong spend their low libido lives at the Chengdu Research Base, located in a mountain region in Western China. I blink away an image of two pandas fucking mid-air, *Crouching Tiger Hidden Dragon* style, on a misty precipice illuminated by floating paper lanterns. After signing my receipt, the seductive scene is replaced with a short narrative of the bitch-owner falling through ice. In my fantasy, I just shrug like my penguin friend.

I ask for a bag just to be a bitch and, of course, it has a smiling fat panda on it. Awesome. She has the nerve to ask, "Anything else?" Initially, I don't say anything. I turn to leave, then I spin around and say, "I'm taking this," picking up a pen from the counter. I walk out twirling the bag on my finger and pocketing the pen, which also has a smiling fat panda on it.

The wet coldness that I felt after leaving the class now feels like a skeletal chill. The music of the wind chime has me thinking of hammocks in the Bahamas. Wouldn't that be sweet? "Waiter! Another mojito please." Writing on the glass window of *Ink Panda,* I address the letter to her workplace, while trying to make sure that I smudge the window of the storefront as much as possible. Can Windex freeze? I really hope so. I have no clue what her real address is. Her current girlfriend and she moved into a new place in June; I just know it's some dirty flat hugging the Slope. When I heard about it, I called and left a voicemail...something about being willing to live anywhere with her...something about even if it was a cardboard box...something about gutters and happiness.

Reading the folded note twice and seeing the tear from my underlined "I'm not," makes me second-guess this move. It's one step up from a note with cut out letters and paste. Jim Carrey's Riddler giggles in my mind. The psychotic missal lands in a trashcan without a sound. I'll go with the $6 penguin card, just not right now. It will be a romantic and cute expression. Definitely a less bat-shit move than the napkin—although, wasn't *Harry Potter* written on napkins? Irrelevant. Maybe, after one more yoga class, I'll be inspired with the right words or the courage to let it go. Actually let her go. Reflexes close my eyes. Instead of making one more gesture, I could fall through the ice of my self-pity. First, shrugging like my penguin, and then accepting the frozen feeling entirely: the complete coldness of separation. My version of *Om Shanti,* i.e. "Peace out, my Love." *Splash*!

You Were Wondering, Perhaps, About Keith Richards?

Susana H. Case

To this day, I cannot look in the mirror without thinking of Keith Richards; the detailed, almost scientific directives that fill his face are difficult to reproduce. Though it isn't mandatory, a more nude Keith Richards seems like something of a rediscovery, a return to an off-camera, everyday realism, a new minimalism, without shading or striping. Recently, I ordered a ravaged copy of Keith Richards, a crucial accessory, just to see if I was exaggerating. There are baroque recipes for combining solids and liquids to create a do-it-yourself Keith Richards, with "three tiny dabs" of different colors to create the right shade of Keith Richards, the part I tend to get wrong. Though I consider myself Keith-Richards savvy, what seems different right now is this piece of advice: use only as many Keith Richards as you feel comfortable with. Wait, you must be thinking, this requires a certain amount of work. There will always be women who want to use Keith Richards as an art installation, but having a good Keith Richards is more important and desirable than how many you pile up. Generally speaking, as one gets older, more is less.

Contributors' Biographies

Michael Alenyikov's first book, "Ivan and Misha," won the 2011 Northern California Book Award for Fiction and was nominated for the Edmund White Award for Debut Fiction. He is the very proud recipient of the 2013 Gina Berriault Award and has been a MacDowell Fellow. His writing has appeared in *The Georgia Review, Descant, The James White Review, New York Stories, Modern Words,* and the *Gay & Lesbian Review*; and has been anthologized in "Best Gay Stories, 2008," and "Best Gay Stories, 2011." He grew up in the outer reaches of New York City's three outer boroughs (and yes, there is an Avenue Z in Brooklyn on the shores of Gravesend Bay). Between the Bronx and Brooklyn, he lived in Phoenix, AZ and Los Angeles, CA. He has worked as a bookstore clerk, clinical psychologist, cab driver, and writer on interactive media projects. In 1989-91 he was on the Board of Directors of the Gay & Lesbian Alliance Against Defamation. After living chunks of years in Syracuse, NY, Boston and Cambridge, MA, and Manhattan, he has made San Francisco his home for the past twenty years. He is one of the one million Americans who suffer from the neuro-immune disease, Myalgic Encephalomyelitis (often called Chronic Fatigue Syndrome), which has crushed the lives of so many people, including countless writers and artists. **A. Anupama** is a U.S.-born, Indian-American poet and translator whose work has appeared in several literary publications, including *The Bitter Oleander, Monkeybicycle, The Alembic,* and *Numéro Cinq Magazine.* She received her MFA in writing from Vermont College of Fine Arts in 2012. She lives in Nyack, New York, and blogs about poetic inspiration at seranam.com. **Hinemoana Baker** lives and writes on the southwest coast of New Zealand's Te Ika-a-Māui/North Island. Her most recent collection, 'kōiwi kōiwi | bone bone', was published in 2010 by Victoria University Press. She works as a writer, editor, musician, teacher and smoking cessation telephone counselor. More information at www.hinemoana.co.nz. **Agatha Beins** lives in Denton, TX, where she teaches women's studies at Texas Woman's University and edits the journal *Films for the Feminist Classroom* when she's not bicycling around town and volunteering at an amazing local farm. Her work appears or is forthcoming in *The Laurel Review, Pebble Lake Review, Newfound, Devil's Lake, Waccamaw, Spiral Orb*, and *Cactus Heart*. **Philip Belcher** has published poetry and critical prose in a variety of literary journals, including *Passages North, Shenandoah, South Dakota Review, Southeast Review, Fugue*, and *The Southern Quarterly*. New poetry and prose are forthcoming in *Asheville Poetry Review, Southern Humanities Review*, and *Bayou Magazine*. In 2007, his chapbook, *The Flies and Their Lovely Names,* was published by Stepping Stones Press at the University of South Carolina. He is an Advisory and Contributing Editor for *Shenandoah* and holds degrees from Furman University, Southeastern Seminary, Duke University School of Law, and Converse College (MFA). He currently serves as Vice President, Programs, of The Community Foundation of Western North Carolina in Asheville, NC. **Lucy Burns** received her BA from Skidmore College with a degree in Spanish and Mathematics. She is currently pursuing her MFA in Poetry at the University of New Mexico, where she serves as the Poetry Editor for *Blue Mesa Review*. **Sean Carswell** is the author of five books. His most recent novel, *Madhouse Fog*, was published by Manic D Press in the summer of 2013. "A Place Called Sickness" is one in a series of short stories he is writing about his favorite authors and their metaphysical ukuleles. Carswell is an assistant professor of writing and literature at California State University Channel Islands. **Susana H. Case** is a professor and program coordinator at the New York Institute of Technology. Her photos have appeared in *San Pedro River Review* and *Blue Hour Magazine*, among others. Author of several chapbooks, her Slapering Hol Press chapbook, *The Scottish Café*, was published in a dual-language version, *Kawiarnia Szkocka*, by Poland's Opole University Press. She authored the books *Salem In Séance* (WordTech Editions), *Elvis Presley's Hips & Mick Jagger's Lips* (Anaphora Literary Press), and *Earth and Below* (Anaphora Literary Press). *4 Rms w Vu* is forthcoming from Mayapple Press in 2014. Please visit her online at: http://iris.nyit.edu/~shcase/. **Christine DeSimone's** first collection, "How Long the Night Is," was published in summer 2013 by Lummox Press. Her poems have appeared or are forthcoming in *Alaska Quarterly Review, Cimarron Review, Cream City Review*, and *Zyzzyva*. She practices law in San Francisco. **Michael**

Dickman was born in Portland, Oregon in 1975, Michael Dickman, his twin brother Matthew, and his younger sister were raised by their mother in the neighborhood of Lents. He received his MFA from the Michener Center for Writers at the University of Texas at Austin. Dickman's first collection, *The End of the West,* was published in 2009 by Copper Canyon Press. He is also the co-author of the forthcoming *50 American Plays* from Copper Canyon Press. His second collection of poetry, *Flies* (Copper Canyon Press, 2011), received the 2010 James Laughlin Award. His many grants, fellowships, and residencies include honors from organizations such as The Michener Center for Writers, The Vermont Studio Center, the Fine Arts Work Center, and the Lannan Foundation. He was awarded the Hodder Fellowship from Princeton University for 2009-2010. In addition to writing, Dickman appeared in the 2002 film *Minority Report* with his twin brother, worked for years as a cook, and has recently been active in the Writers in the Schools program. See more at: http://www.poets.org/poet.php/prmPID/1839#sthash.ODMChWYk.dpuf. **Daniel Donaghy** is the author of two poetry collections: *Start with the Trouble* (University of Arkansas Press, 2009) and *Streetfighting* (2005). He has work in recent or forthcoming issues of *Antioch Review, Sou'wester, Notre Dame Review,* and *Nimrod.* "Hood Ghazal" is from a manuscript in progress entitled "Somerset." **Molly Faerber's** work has appeared or is forthcoming in *Harpur Palate, Wigleaf,* and *Keyhole Magazine.* She lives, writes, and teaches in Providence, RI where she is pursuing an MFA in fiction writing from Brown University. **Matthew Fogarty**, born and raised in the square-mile suburbs of Detroit, currently lives and writes in Columbia, where he is fiction editor of *Yemassee.* He also edits *Cartagena*, a literary journal. His fiction has appeared or is forthcoming in such journals as *Revolution House, FRiGG, Midwestern Gothic, JMWW,* and *Moon City Review.* He can be found at http://www.matthewfogarty.com. **Jeannine Hall Gailey** recently served as the Poet Laureate of Redmond, Washington and is the author of three books of poetry: *Becoming the Villainess* (Steel Toe Books, 2006) *She Returns to the Floating World* (Kitsune Books, 2011) and *Unexplained Fevers,* just out from New Binary Press. Her work has been featured on *NPR's The Writer's Almanac, Verse Daily,* and in *The Year's Best Fantasy and Horror*. Her poems have appeared in *The American Poetry Review, The Iowa Review* and *Prairie Schooner*. Her website is www.webbish6.com. **Trina Gaynon** is a graduate of the Creative Writing program at University of San Francisco. Her poems appear in the anthologies *Bombshells* and *Knocking at the Door*, as well as numerous journals including *Natural Bridge, Reed* and the final issue of *Runes*. Her chapbook *An Alphabet of Romance* is available from Finishing Line Press. Poems in forthcoming anthologies: *A Ritual to Read Together: Poems in Conversation with William Stafford, Saint Peter's B-list: Contemporary Poems Inspired by the Saints, Obsession: Sestinas for the 21st Century,* and *Phoenix Rising from the Ashes: Anthology of Sonnets of the Early Third Millennium*. http://tdgaynon.webs.com/. **Heather June Gibbons'** poems have appeared recently in *Boston Review, Forklift, Ohio, West Branch, The Cincinnati Review,* and *Indiana Review,* and she is the author of the chapbook *Flyover* (Q Ave Press, 2012). A graduate of the Iowa Writers' Workshop, she teaches creative writing at San Francisco State University. **Carol Gore** is originally from Whiteville, NC, home of poet A.R. Ammons, lots of farms, and not much else. She holds an MFA in writing from the California College of the Arts in San Francisco, CA. Currently, she resides in Raleigh, NC with her husband, son, and Pekingese. **Ivan Hobson** is a graduate of San Francisco State University's MFA program. He is also a fourth generation machinist, working with his dad in the small shop his great-grandfather built in 1935. Ivan's poetry has recently appeared, or is forthcoming, in publications including *The North American Review, The Fourth River, California Quarterly*, and Ted Kooser's weekly "American Life in Poetry" column. **Dustin M. Hoffman** spent ten years painting houses in Michigan before getting his MFA in fiction from Bowling Green State University and his PhD in creative writing from Western Michigan University. His stories have appeared in *The Masters Review, Phoebe, Puerto del Sol, Witness, Quarterly West, Copper Nickel, Gargoyle, Fifth Wednesday Journal, Indiana Review,* and a bunch of other neat places. His chapbook *Secrets of the Wild* is forthcoming with Burning River Press. He lives in Kalamazoo and is a visiting assistant professor at Albion College. Visit his little online home at http://dustinmhoffman.wordpress.com/. **Michael Jones** teaches at

Oakland High School in Oakland, CA. His work has appeared recently in *Beloit Poetry Journal* and is forthcoming in *Tar River Poetry*. **Mary Julia Klimenko** has an MA in Creative Writing from SFSU and has been writing poetry and short stories for forty years. She is also a psychotherapist in private practice. She lives in Vallejo, California. In addition to publication in many literary journals, she has a book in print, *SOURCE VEIN*, published by Spire Press and three limited edition books in print created in collaboration with sculptor Manuel Neri. **Dan Langton** is author of *Querencia,* University of Missouri Press (Devins Award), 1975; *The Inheritance*, a play produced by the Julian Theatre, 1980; *The Hogarth-Selkirk Letters*, 1985; *Life Forms*, Cheltenham Press, 1995; *Greatest Hits,* 2000; *The Sonnets*, 2005; *During Our Walks,* 2012. Poems in *Three Penny Review, Atlantic Monthly, Paris Review, The Nation, The American Scholar, The Iowa Review*, and other magazines and journals. Winner of the Devins Award for Poetry, the Hart Crane Award, the London Prize, the Browning Award, the Edgar Allan Poe Memorial Award, and the Roberts Prize. **David Dodd Lee** has published seven previous full-length books of poems, including *Orphan, Indiana* (Akron, 2010), *The Nervous Filaments* (Four Way Books, 2010), *Abrupt Rural* (New Issues, 2004) and *Downsides of Fish Culture* (New Issues, 1979). *Sky Booths in the Breath Somewhere, The Ashbery Erasure Poems* (BlazeVox, 2010) appeared as well in 2010. His newest book, *The Coldest Winter On Earth*, Poems 1998-2011, appeared in 2012 from Marick Press. His eighth book, *Animalities,* will be published by Four Way Books in 2014. Lee now lives and fishes just south of the Michigan border, on a river in northern Indiana. He is currently an assistant professor of English at Indiana University South Bend. **Meredith Luby** is from Virginia. She lives in Rhode Island where she is an MFA candidate at Brown University. Her work has previously appeared in *Redivider* and *Glimmer Train.* **Farzana Marie** is a poet and PhD student at the University of Arizona, where she focuses on Persian Literature and Creative Writing. She is a U.S. Air Force veteran and has spent three years in Afghanistan in both military and civilian roles. Farzana's poetry has appeared in print and on-line journals including *The Rusty Nail, Adanna, Exit Strata, When Women Waken*, and *Subprimal Poetry Art,* as well as forthcoming anthologies by Holy Cow! Press and Fantastic Books. She authored the nonfiction book *Hearts for Sale! A Buyer's Guide to Winning in Afghanistan*. Find her on Twitter @farzanamarie. **Kevin McLellan** is the author of the chapbooks *Shoes on a Wire* (Split Oak, forthcoming), runner-up for the 2012 Stephen Dunn Prize in Poetry, and *Round Trip* (Seven Kitchens, 2010), a collaborative series of poems with numerous women poets. He has recent or forthcoming poems in books and journals including: *2014 Poets Market, American Letters & Commentary, Barrow Street, Colorado Review, Hawaii Review, Kenyon Review Online, Sixth Finch, Western Humanities Review, Witness,* and numerous others. Kevin lives in Cambridge, MA, and sometimes teaches poetry workshops at the University of Rhode Island in Providence. **Christopher J. Michel** is a writer and stay-at-home-dad, living in Brooklyn's secret Chinatown. He loves running, cooking, and watching his three-year-old daughter scooter around in the park near his house. His work has been published or is forthcoming in *Juked, Barrow Street, Summerset Review,* and *Stone Canoe*. He has been twice nominated for a Pushcart Prize. He can be reached at christopher.j.michel@gmail.com. **James Norcliffe**, New Zealand poet, has published eight collections of poetry, most recently *Villon in Millerton* in 2007 and *Shadow Play in* 2013. He has also published fiction including a number of fantasy novels for young readers, most recently the award-winning *The Loblolly Boy* published in the US as *The Boy Who Could Fly* (Egmont USA). Recent work has appeared in *Spillway, The Cincinnati Review, Salamander* and *Gargoyle.* In 2010, he took part in the XX International Poetry Festival in Medellín, Colombia and in 2013 the Trois-Rivières International Poetry Festival in Quebec. **David O'Connell's** chapbook, *A Better Way to Fall,* was awarded the 2013 Philbrick Poetry Award. His work has appeared in *Columbia Poetry Review, Drunken Boat, Fugue,* and *Poet Lore*, among other journals. **Darlene Pagán** teaches writing and literature at Pacific University in Oregon. She has a chapbook of poems, *Blue Ghosts* (Finishing Line Press) and poems and essays in many journals, including *Field, Calyx, Hayden's Ferry Review, Poet Lore, Hiram Poetry Review, Brevity, Lake Effect,* and *Hawaii Pacific Review.* She is a poetry editor for *VoiceCatcher* and a member of the writer's group Broads on the Side. She enjoys hiking, biking, the beach, the rain, and carnival rides now that her sons are just tall enough to ride. **Jared Pearce** teaches literature and writing at William Penn University. His poems have recently been published in *The Deronda Review, Of(f) Course, Hospital Drive, Tiger Train*, and *Marco Polo*. **Mimi Plevin-Foust's** poetry, screenplays and articles have been or will be published by *Forge Journal, LearnVest.com, POZ Magazine, SCRIPT, Spoon River Poetry Review, Stickman Review, Willow Review* and more. She received her MFA from NYU's Dramatic Writing program. Mimi produced and directed the widely screened documentaries, *'Wide Time: An HIV Odyssey'* and *'Hopes and Fears: Rusti's Story'*, two films about long-term AIDS survivors and their secrets for making life not only long—but wide. **Alexis Pope** is the author of three chapbooks, *alive & forthcoming*. Her work has appeared or is forthcoming in *Guernica, Washington Square, RHINO*, and *Inter|rupture,* among others. Her first collection was selected for the Joanna Cargill First Book Award & will be published by Coconut Books in 2014. She lives in Brooklyn with a boy + baby. **Nick Francis Potter** is a multimedia artist and writer from Salt Lake City, Utah. His work has appeared most recently (probably) in *Sleepingfish, Black Warrior Review, Bat City Review, The Chattahoochee Review*, and online at *Hobart*, among others. He currently lives in Columbia, MO with his wife and two sons. His tumblr is nickfrancispotter.tumblr.com. **Jane Rose Porter** is a 2013 Emerging Writer Fellow with the Center for Fiction in New York. She has published essays and articles in *The Kenyon Review, The Wall Street Journal, BusinessWeek Magazine, Men's Health, Entrepreneur,* and *The Chronicle of Higher Education.* She was awarded a Jentel Artist Residency and is a graduate of the Warren Wilson MFA Program for Writers. Jane has a B.A. in English from Brown University, where she was a Rose Writing Fellow. She lives in Brooklyn and is completing her first novel. **Daniel Riddle Rodriguez's** real name is Daniel Riddle Rodriguez. He is a part-time student, full-time construction worker from San Lorenzo, California, where he lives with his son. Previous publications include *Danse Macabre*, and *Monkeybicycle.* He is thrilled to be here. **Kate Scarpetta** is a professional golfer who currently resides in Orlando, FL. She graduated from Princeton with a B.A. in English and received an award from the Creative Writing Department for her work. Her stories have appeared in *The Brooklyn Review, The Coachella Review, Word Riot*, and *SplitLip*. More of Kate's writing can be found on her website: www.katescarpetta.com. **Ray Shea's** writing has appeared in *Sundog Lit, ARDOR, Connotation Press, The Rumpus,* and elsewhere. A native of Boston and New Orleans, he currently lives in Austin. **Noel Sloboda's** work has recently appeared in *Rattle, Harpur Palate, Redactions*, and *Modern Language Studies*. He is the author of the poetry collections *Shell Games* (2008) and *Our Rarer Monsters* (2013) as well as several chapbooks. Sloboda has also published a book about Edith Wharton and Gertrude Stein. He serves as dramaturg for the Harrisburg Shakespeare Company and teaches at Penn State York. **John Warner Smith** is a Cave Canem fellow whose poems have appeared in or are forthcoming in *Ploughshares, Callaloo, The Worcester Review, Pembroke, Kestrel, African American Review, American Athenaeum* and other literary journals. His short collection, "Hunting Dragonflies," was a finalist in the 2012 poetry competition of the Tennessee Williams / New Orleans Literary Festival. A resident of Baton Rouge, Louisiana, he directs a statewide organization dedicated to improving public education. He also teaches English and African American Literature at Southern University in Baton Rouge. He earned his MFA at the University of New Orleans. **Patricia Canright Smith** writes fiction, memoir, and personal essays from her home in Seattle, Washington. "The Lucky" is from a collection of linked stories with human/animal intersections: condors, spiders, pythons, wallabies, rats, a feral cat, gnats. The stories consider the solace of the natural world—or not. She's curious why people do what they do, compelled to watch and describe what she sees. Usually this means delving into the ordinary: a man's emptiness, a widow's shift, an artist's aphasia. It means addressing unacknowledged fractures between races, genders, and generations. She also creates visual art in various mediums and sometimes images find their way into the narratives. Until recently, she practiced psychotherapy as well. Her work has appeared in anthologies and journals, including *Short Story America* (third prize), the *Jabberwock Review* and *Catamaran Literary Reader*. www.patriciacanrightsmith.com. **Meghan Tifft** received her MFA from the University of Arizona. She currently teaches creative writing at the University of Colorado in Colorado Springs. **Michelle Valois** lives in western Massachusetts with her partner and their three children. Her writing has appeared in *TriQuarterly, The Massachusetts Review, Pank, Brevity, Fourth Genre, The Baltimore Review,* and others. She teaches writing and humanities at a community college and blogs at http://www.readmelikeabook.net/. "Nursemaids" is from *Lost Gods and Hungry Sailors,* which will be published in early 2014 by Big Table Publishing. **Rodney Wilhite** is an MFA graduate of the University of Arkansas. His work has appeared in or is forthcoming in *Pleiades, Splash of Red, Cartographer,* and *The Puritan.* He lives in Fayetteville with his wife and five-month-old daughter. **Ruth Williams**, in addition to her poetry chapbook, *Conveyance* (Dancing Girl Press, 2012), her poetry and creative nonfiction has appeared in literary journals such as *jubilat, DIAGRAM, Cutbank, Third Coast, alice blue, South Loop Review* and *Faultline.* Currently, she is an assistant professor of English at William Jewell College. **Terita Heath-Wlaz** is a writer and teacher. Her poems have appeared in *New Letters, Pank, Cream City Review, Court Green*, and others. She holds an MFA from the University of Florida, and lives on Long Island with her partner and their son. **Vincent Craig Wright** is a short story and songwriter from Ashland, Oregon. Professor of Creative Writing at Southern Oregon University and Co-Founder of the Institute of New Writing/Ashland, he has recent work in *BlazeVox, Sleet Magazine, The Harvard Advocate* and a book of stories, *Redemption Center* (Bear Star Press). **Carina Yun** is a native San Franciscan and has obtained an MS degree in Software Engineering from CSU Fullerton. She studied Poetry at Northern Virginia Community College, the Jenny McKean Moore Writers' Workshop, and Bread Loaf Writers' Conference. She is currently working on completing her poetry manuscript, *The Green Umbrella.* Some of her poems have appeared/are forthcoming in *Calliope* and *Poet Lore Magazine.* She currently lives, works, and writes in Northern Virginia.

The Editors would like to thank the following bookstores for carrying *Fourteen Hills*:

In the Bay Area:

Adobe Books
Aardvark Books
Alexander Books Co.
Bibliohead
Bird and Becket
Books and Bookshelves
Books, Inc.
The Booksmith
Bound Together Books
Christopher's Books
City Lights
Diesel
Dog Eared Books
Farley's East
Farley's on 65th
Farley's West
Green Apple
Issues
Modern Times
Needles & Pens
Phoenix Books
Revolution Books
SFSU Bookstore
Smoke Signals
Spoonbill & Sugartown
University Press Books
USF Bookstore
Walden Pond Books
West Portal Bookshop

In California:

Book Soup :: Los Angeles
Bookshop Benicia :: Benicia
Bookshop Santa Cruz :: Santa Cruz
Kepler's :: Menlo Park
Last Bookstore :: Los Angeles
Main Street Books :: Los Altos
Paras News :: San Diego
Newsbeat :: Davis
Reader's Books :: Sonoma
Skylight Books :: Los Angeles
Watershed Books :: Lakeport
William Jessup University :: Rocklin

Across the U.S. and Beyond:

A Cappella Books :: Atlanta, GA
Atomic Books :: Baltimore, MD
Avril 50 :: Philadelphia, PA
Book Corner :: Bloomington, IN
Book People :: Austin, TX
Brookline Booksmith :: Brookline, MA
Duant Books :: London, UK
The Elliott Bay Book Company :: Seattle, WA
Hudson News Grand Central :: New York, NY
Ink On A :: New York, NY
Kay's Magazine Plus, Inc. :: New York, NY
Magazine Cafe :: New York, NY
Magpies Newstand Cafe :: Durango, CO
Malaprops :: Asheville, NC
McNally Jackson Books :: New York, NY
Politics and Prose :: Washington, DC
Powell's Books :: Portland, OR
Prairie Lights :: Iowa City, IA
Quimby's Books :: Chicago, IL
Regulator Bookshop :: Durham, NC
St. Marks Books :: New York, NY
Tattered Cover Books Cherry Creek :: Denver, CO
Women and Children First :: Chicago, IL
Writer's Center :: Chicago, IL
Writer's Center :: Bethesda, MD

PANK
www.pankmagazine.com

the
Folio
UC BERKELEY'S UNDERGRADUATE ENGLISH JOURNAL
"The Folio" is a publication of the UC Berkeley English Undergraduate Association. We publish short literary analysis essays written by Berkeley undergraduates every spring. To order a copy of "The Folio" send your mailing address and $5 to
The Folio
400 Eshleman Hall MC# 4500
Berkeley, CA, 94720-4500, United States.
www.ocf.berkeley.edu/~thefolio

Camera
Obscura
Journal of Literature
& Photography
micro
short story
novella
traditional
experimental
imaginative
Photography competition deadlines:
Sept. 15 - Winter
March 15 - Summer
Open to Amateur and Professionals
Camera Obscura is found at bookstores nationwide
OR
Subscribe online:
www.ObscuraJournal.com
Featured in Best Magazines of 2010
The Library Journal - May 2011
"Camera Obscura is a well-edited compilation of fine fiction and photography worth considering for collections of contemporary American literature."
-Library Journal
"Camera Obscura is the kind of publication that will definitely keep readers demanding print publications they can hold in their hands."
-NewPages Blog
A Biannual Exhibition of Contemporary Prose & Photography
www.obscurajournal.com

1111:
Writing
and Art that
Dances!
Submit!
Eleven Eleven: A Journal of Literature and Art
California College of the Arts
1111 Eighth Street
San Francisco, California 94107
elevenelevenjournal.com

Fourteen Hills Press

presents

NIAGARA TRANSNATIONAL

by Sarah Heady

Winner of the 2013 Michael Rubin First Book Award

Sarah Heady's Niagara Transnational is an epic American travelogue, but don't expect mythic vistas and fruited plains. Heady, our 21st-century Virgil, propels us with gutsy, erotic, punky aplomb into the rusted waste and sugary spoils of the last century. With this series of sagely annotated poems made of passionate trash—old postcards, out-of-date informational placards, crumbling amusement park rides, rest stop confessions—Heady reports to us from the field. In Heady's newborn folk song we hear the traveller who resists being fully a stranger, as if true wandering can only take place at home on familiar roads. And as readers we too come to own this place.

— Barbara Tomash

Purchase copies from Small Press Distribution: www.spd.org

Subscribe to Fourteen Hills

Prices include shipping and handling.

Single issue (current): $9

One Year (two issues): $15

Two Years (four issues): $28

Institutional (one year): $17

Back Issues (please specify): $5

Subscribe online at www.14hills.net

Fourteen Hills
Department of Creative Writing
San Francisco State University
1600 Holloway Avenue
San Francisco, CA 94132-1722